General
Equilibrium
Analysis

General Equilibrium Analysis

An Introduction

David Simpson

BASIL BLACKWELL
OXFORD

ISBN 0 631 16210 0

981482

Printed and bound in Great Britain
by William Clowes & Sons Limited, London,
Colchester and Beccles

To my Father and Mother

Contents

Preface

This book is written for third-year undergraduates and post-graduate students who feel the need for a simple but comprehensive exposition of general equilibrium analysis. Despite the prevalence of general equilibrium analysis throughout modern economic theory, I have been aware of the lack of a suitable textbook. Phelps Brown's excellent pre-war volume is out of print, and most books which are now on the market assume a knowledge of mathematics beyond that of the average student of economics. It seemed as if there might be a place for a book which provides an introduction to the analysis, while remaining accessible to students with no more than a basic knowledge of calculus and linear algebra. Keeping the mathematics simple necessarily rules out detailed discussion of such issues as the existence, uniqueness and stability of solutions, but permits a full account of what are, in my opinion, the more interesting aspects of general equilibrium.

Very few of the ideas in the book are novel: as I have tried to indicate by references throughout the text, most can be found in other publications. If the book has any claim to originality it is in the arrangement of the material, which is designed to emphasise the underlying unity of many of the major branches of economic theory – those which have evolved from the theory of value. At the same time, I hope that the book makes clear the limitations of general equilibrium analysis in dealing with such topics as long-run growth and development, money and the trade cycle.

The book reflects to a certain extent the influences of my teachers, and I have been privileged to have been taught by a number of inspiring people. I should like to take the opportunity to acknowledge the encouragement I have received from two of them, Wassily Leontief and Alan

Peacock. I should also like to thank the students at the University of Stirling from whose critical remarks this book has benefited. Paul Hare and David Ulph were kind enough to give a critical reading to an earlier draft which resulted in several improvements. I am indebted to other colleagues at Stirling, including A D Bain, C V Brown, M A Grieg, J W McGilvray and D J Taylor for their helpful suggestions. At least two drafts of the manuscript were patiently typed by Mrs Sheelagh Blackhall and Mrs Andrine Rocks. The responsibility for any remaining deficiencies is mine.

Dunblane, Perthshire.
January, 1975   DAVID SIMPSON

Introduction

The Theory of Value has traditionally been at the centre of economic theorising, and the modern treatment of the subject through general equilibrium analysis emphasises the essential duality of pricing and resource allocation. A second reason for attaching importance to general equilibrium analysis is that it represents the interdependence of different parts of an economic system. But perhaps the most important reason for wishing to study general equilibrium analysis is that it provides a unifying framework within which some major branches of economic theory can be related. The Theory of Value, Welfare Economics, the Pure Theory of International Trade, and the Theory of Economic Growth can all be shown to have a common origin. Above all, the gulf between microeconomics and macroeconomics which is bewildering to the average student is easily bridged. As opposed to the view that it is a collection of disparate tools, our approach in this book emphasises the essential unity of economic analysis.

What is General Equilibrium Analysis?

In *general* equilibrium analysis the interdependence of the prices and quantities of all the commodities and factors in the economy is explicitly recognised. In the solution of a general equilibrium system the set of prices of commodities and factors as well as the quantities of goods produced and factors used by each firm and the quantities of goods consumed and factors supplied by each household are simultaneously determined. Because there exists a very large number of firms, households and commodities in any economic system it is common to undertake what is called a *partial* equilibrium analysis. In this approach, attention is focused on a small number of variables and relationships, typically those relating to a single commodity, while the remainder of the variables and relationships in the economic system is ignored. For example, the quantities supplied and demanded of a commodity such as sugar are assumed to be functions of the price of sugar alone. The possible influence of changes in the prices of other commodities and factors upon the supply and demand for sugar is ignored.

Thus, partial equilibrium analysis can be regarded as one way of simplifying a system of general economic equilibrium. An alternative method of simplification is to aggregate the variables in such a way that a single aggregate commodity is produced by the aggregate of firms and consumed by the aggregate of households. Relationships between such aggregate variables form the subject of *macroeconomic* theory.

A choice between each of these three methods for analysing the economic system depends entirely upon the appropriateness of each to the particular question which is being posed.

For example, to use a general equilibrium analysis to try to answer a question concerning the likely effect of a 10% rise in the price of sugar upon the quantity of sugar demanded would be to complicate the answer unnecessarily. On the other hand, a partial equilibrium analysis would be quite inadequate to deal with a question concerning the effect upon the prices of different commodities of a 10% rise in the wage-rate throughout every sector of the economy.

This point can be illustrated by means of an analogy. A church may be denoted by a cross on an ordnance survey map, but it may also be described in greater detail in a guidebook. A map is more useful than a guidebook if one is interested in the location of objects in a landscape, but not if one is interested in church architecture. Likewise a general equilibrium analysis is more useful if one wants to explore the consequences of the interdependence of the various sectors of an economy, but it is less useful if one is interested in only a single sector.

What is Equilibrium?

We have distinguished between a *partial* and a *general* equilibrium analysis: what then, is an *equilibrium* analysis?

Hansen (1970) defines the concept of equilibrium in the following way:

if we have an economic model that explains certain variables, and if there is no tendency for these variables to change, given the data of the model, then the system of variables is in equilibrium.

In the simplest case of economic equilibrium, the case of the single market, the market is said to be in equilibrium if the quantity supplied equals the quantity demanded. But this explanation is deceptively simple: implicit in it are assumptions about the behaviour of the system if the quantities supplied and demanded are *not* equal. The meaning of equilibrium is explored in chapter 6. Meanwhile, it is only necessary to make two points.

First of all, as we shall see in chapters 9 and 10 equilibrium solutions very often have certain *efficiency* properties.

Secondly, while this book is to be largely devoted to the traditional static equilibrium analysis, the concept of equilibrium is in no way incompatible with an evolutionary state of the world. For example in equilibrium models of economic growth, the absolute value of all the variables increases over time.

Because of the prevalence of static analysis in economic theory and because of the efficiency properties of equilibrium, there is a widespread but fallacious belief that general equilibrium theory presumes that the world is (or should be) in a state of harmony, in some ill-defined sense. In fact, equilibrium analysis, as we shall show, is consistent with a variety of states of the world, many of which would be considered unacceptable by most people. For example, an equilibrium solution might include wage rates for some types of labour which were well below subsistence level. Equilibrium analysis is a *method* of economic theory, and the use of that method does not, by itself, justify inferences about the nature of the world. The use of equilibrium methods can be justified simply by pointing out that very much more complicated methods are required in a disequilibrium analysis—i.e. when we deal with the out-of-equilibrium behaviour of an economic model.

Classical and Neoclassical Theory

We have divided our treatment of general equilibrium analyses into three parts: in Parts I and II of the book we adopt neoclassical methods and assumptions and in Part III we use classical methods and assumptions. By "classical" we refer to that tradition which begins with Adam Smith and which can be traced through Ricardo and Marx to

Leontief and von Neumann, while by "neoclassical" we refer to the line of thought, also originating with Smith, which runs from Walras to Debreu. Classical general equilibrium analysis is characterised by limited substitutability in production and consumption, by having a separate theory of distribution, and pays slight attention to the role of demand. Limited substitutability is usually represented by linear relationships which lend themselves to empirical estimation. Neoclassical analysis, on the other hand, emphasises substitution possibilities, and is therefore represented by continuous functions, which are generally non-operational. The prices of factors in neoclassical analysis are determined, like commodity prices, within the model. Unlike the classical analysis, the neoclassical is founded upon explicit assumptions concerning the behaviour of individual producers and consumers.

Plan of the Book

The basic components of a neoclassical general equilibrium system are derived from first principles in chapters 1 to 4, which deal with the theories of consumption, production, and markets. These components are put together in chapter 5 to form a complete system. This chapter also includes a numerical example designed to illustrate the significance of such a system. The meaning of existence, uniqueness and stability conditions for neoclassical systems is outlined in chapter 6.

The possibility of integrating money into the system is discussed in chapter 7, while Keynes' criticisms are considered in chapter 8. The system built up in the first five chapters requires little modification to act as a basis for the exposition of the principles of welfare economics in chapter 9. Confidence in the prescriptive power of welfare economics has been shaken by Impossibility theorems such as those of Arrow and the Second Best. These and other complications are considered in chapter 10.

By extending the now familiar framework of analysis from one economy to two, the pure theory of international trade can be presented in its neoclassical version, (chapter 11). But this is about as far as the neoclassical analysis can usefully be carried. Its limitations from an operational point of view are obvious. Less elegant but more robust general equilibrium systems may be constructed from alternative assumptions, and the principal differences and similarities between classical and neoclassical systems are discussed in chapter 12. The remaining chapters are devoted to elaborating classical systems in order of increasing generality. Appropriately we can begin with Adam Smith, in whose "golden age" the labour theory of value holds unquestioned sway (chapter 13). Leontief's static input–output system may be regarded as a multi-sectoral elaboration of Smith's system, and some empirical applications of this system as well as its theoretical properties are described.

The possibility of choice of technology is introduced in chapter 14, first in a two-sector Ricardian model, and then in a multi-sectoral version. Finally, in the last two chapters the constraint of the single time period is relaxed. The transition to a dynamic system reveals not only that the valuation/allocation duality still holds but that some interesting new duality properties appear as well.

A Note on Method

At least five different methods have been used in economics textbooks and in the journals to expound the theory of value. Each method is loosely associated with a particular school of writers.

Thus, (a) purely *literary methods* were favoured by the classical economists such as Smith and Ricardo, while it is to Marshall that we we owe the introduction of (b) *geometric* (i.e. diagrammatic) methods. The use of (c) the *calculus* in economic theory has grown with the influence of neoclassical theory. More recently the post-war development of activity analysis has led to the popularisation of (d) *linear algebra* as a vehicle for economic theory, and this is quite closely related to the use of (e) *set theoretic* methods by Arrow, Debreu and others in proving theorems concerning the existence of general equilibrium solutions.

Each of these methods is an alternative, and which is used depends on the purpose on hand. Method (e) is the one best suited to advancing rigorous proofs from well-defined assumptions but it may not be the best way to understand certain economic principles. In this book, we shall rely mainly on (a) and (c) in Parts I and II, and (a) and (d) in Part III, but we shall resort to (b) from time to time throughout the book.

Some Preliminary Considerations

While particular assumptions are spelled out in the appropriate chapters, there are some more general assumptions which may be presumed to prevail throughout the book, except where otherwise stated.

(i) *Institutions*. The analysis is independent of any particular set of institutional arrangements: in particular, it does not matter whether the non-human factors of production are privately or socially owned. The economic system, however, must be a decentralised one and not a purely command economy. In such an economy, the central authority, if perfectly informed, could merely allocate resources by *fiat*. But so long as economic decisions remain primarily in the hands of individual households and enterprises (as is the case in all real-world economies), it does not matter, from the point of view of our analysis, whether the prices which the decision-making units take as given to them are established by some market mechanism, by computational process, or by some other means.

(ii) *Time*. Our method of analysis is, in general, a static one, although we use a dynamic analysis in discussing the question of stability in chapter 6, and both chapters 15 and 16 are devoted to dynamic systems of general equilibrium. A static analysis may be defined as one in which all the relationships are assumed to work themselves out within a single period of time. This assumption generally rules out consideration of investment, which may be regarded as a process which consumes goods in one period of time and produces goods in a future period. A comparative static analysis compares two situations before and after an hypothesised change in an exogenous variable: it does not, however, analyse the process by which the system moves from the old to the new situation. To do this requires a dynamic analysis.

(iii) *Money*. It is assumed that money does not exist as a separate commodity but only as an accounting unit. This assumption is relaxed in chapter 7, where money as a commodity is introduced into the general equilibrium system.

(iv) *Interdependence among Producers and Consumers* other than that specified in the mechanism of production and exchange is excluded. This assumption rules out what are usually known as external economies and diseconomies in production and consumption. For example, individual households are assumed *not* to be influenced in their purchasing behaviour by their neighbour's purchases. Nor can pollution of the atmosphere by one producer be assumed to affect the wellbeing of any consumer or the profits of any other producer. This assumption is made for simplicity; it does not mean that problems such as pollution cannot be handled in a general equilibrium analysis.

(v) *Tastes, Factor Supplies and Technology* are all assumed to remain unchanged unless otherwise stated.

(vi) *Foreign Trade* and international factor movements are ruled out. We assume a closed economy. This assumption is relaxed in chapter 11, where our analysis is extended to the case of two countries trading with each other.

(vii) *Public goods*, i.e. those commodities which have a zero opportunity cost of consumption, lead to some difficulties in a general equilibrium analysis. These and other complications are considered in chapter 10. Elsewhere, we assume that all goods are private goods.

(viii) *Intermediate goods.* It is usual in neoclassical analysis to assume that primary inputs, supplied by households, are transformed into final goods, consumed by households. This is a convention which we follow in Parts I and II. The exclusion of intermediate goods is a matter of simplification, and involves no loss of generality.

(ix) *Prices and quantities* can take only non-negative values. This assumption rules out the possibility of meaningless solutions, and it implies that useless by-products can be disposed of costlessly.

Notation

The following notation is used throughout the book. Additional notation is introduced in particular chapters where it is necessary.

q_i = quantity of good i demanded by final consumers
q_{ik} = quantity of good i demanded by consumer k
x_i = quantity of good i supplied by producers
x_i^f = quantity of good i supplied by producer f
p_i = price per unit of good i
z_k = income or expenditure of consumer k

y_j = quantity of input of factor j

y_{ji} = quantity of input of factor j used in the production of good i

r_j = price per unit of input of factor j

a_{ij} = quantity of good or input i used per unit of output of good or activity j

$\bar{y}_{jk}$ = quantity of factor i held by consumer k

PART I

Foundations of a Neoclassical General Equilibrium System

1 Theory of Consumption

From the theory of consumer behaviour we can derive the first component of our general equilibrium system—the demand function for a commodity. The demand function simply states that the quantity of any commodity purchased by a consumer is dependent on the set of prices of all commodities and the income of the consumer. In this chapter we shall show how such a demand function can be formally derived from some simple assumptions concerning consumer behaviour. We begin by discussing these assumptions.

Let it be assumed initially that the prices of commodities are given to the individual consumer, and that his money income is fixed.[1] The problem is how to determine the quantities of each commodity he will choose to consume. The possibility of saving and borrowing having been ruled out by our single time period assumption (see Introduction), the consumer's income will be entirely devoted to his purchases.[2]

The consumer is assumed to have a knowledge of all possible alternative combinations of commodities and to be capable of ranking them in order of his preference for them (his "tastes"). If he can do this he is said to act "rationally". More precisely this postulate of rationality is contained in the three following assumptions:

(i) *Completeness*: For all possible pairs, A and B, of alternative

---

[1] This is only a preliminary assumption. As we shall see when we put together a complete general equilibrium system in chapter 5, the set of prices and the income of each consumer become variables whose values are to be determined. In a partial equilibrium analysis, on the other hand, the income of each consumer and all prices but one are treated as parameters.

[2] The nonsatiation assumption (see p. 2 below), rules out the possibility of some of the consumer's income remaining unspent.

commodity combinations, the consumer knows whether he
prefers A to B or B to A or whether he is indifferent between
them.

(ii) *Transitivity*: If there are three commodity combinations A, B
and C, and if the consumer prefers A to B and B to C then he
must prefer A to C.

(iii) *Nonsatiation*: For any combination of commodities there must
exist another which is preferred to it.

The consumer can be imagined to arrive at his decision as to how much
of each commodity he should purchase by the simple process of
starting at the top of his ranking of all possible commodity
combinations of an equal value, say £10, and working his way down
until his income is exhausted. However, the process of choice may be
formalised slightly differently, in a way which lends itself to treatment
with calculus.

Let us suppose that a number, to be called a utility index number, is
attached to each commodity combination such as A or B or C. The
only requirement which is imposed upon the choice of numbers is that
higher numbers must correspond to preferred combinations and lower
numbers to less preferred combinations. It is essential to avoid thinking
that combination A is preferred to B because A has the higher utility: it
is *because* A is preferred to B that we assign A the higher utility index
number. When he has made his choice of commodities, the consumer
will find that he has simultaneously attained that value of his utility
index which is the maximum possible within the limits imposed by the
size of his income. This may be formalised by saying that the consumer
acts as if he maximises the value of his utility function subject to his
income constraint.

The process of maximising one function subject to the constraint of
another is familiar in economics, and well-known formal methods exist
for its solution. However, in order to guarantee the existence of a
unique solution which is meaningful in economic terms we must make
two further assumptions which limit the acceptable forms[3] of the
utility function.

(iv) *Substitutability*: If there are two combinations A and B, each
containing the same amount of commodity 1 and B has less of

[3] Assumptions (i) to (v) restrict the acceptable forms of the utility
function to those which, if illustrated graphically in cross-section,
would reveal a system of well-behaved indifference curves.

commodity 2, and if A is preferred to B, then assumption (iv) states that there exists some finite amount of commodity 1 which can be added to B so that it will become indifferent to A.

(v) *Convexity*: The more one has of any one commodity, the utility index remaining constant, the lower will be the rate of substitution of any other commodity for it.

The rate of substitution in consumption, hereafter denoted as RSC, between two commodities i and j may be defined as the number of units of i required to compensate the consumer for the loss of one unit of j. It is also defined by the ratio of the corresponding partial derivatives of the utility function, f_i and f_j.

Taken together assumptions (i) to (v) provide sufficient conditions for the existence of a maximum value of the utility function, given the consumer's budget constraint.

The demand function can now be derived in the following way. We wish to attain the highest value of the utility function consistent with the consumer's limited income. Denoting the quantity of good i consumed by the kth consumer as q_{ik}, and assuming that there are n commodities we can write the utility function of the kth consumer as

$$U_k = f_k(q_{1k}, q_{2k}, \ldots, q_{nk}) \tag{1.1}$$

and, denoting the consumer's income by z_k, we can write the income constraint as

$$z_k - \sum_{i=1}^{n} p_i q_{ik} = 0 \tag{1.2}$$

Maximising the utility function subject to this constraint is equivalent to finding the maximum value of the expression

$$V = f_k(q_{1k}, q_{2k}, \ldots, q_{nk}) + \lambda \left(z_k - \sum_{i=1}^{n} p_i q_{ik} \right) \tag{1.3}$$

where λ is a so-called Lagrangean multiplier.[4] To understand this procedure, notice that for those values of q_{ik} that satisfy the constraint (1.2)—and those are the only values of q_{ik} that we are interested in—then V is identically equivalent to U.

[4] λ can simply be regarded as an additional unknown variable. There is a particular value of λ which will guarantee that the maximum value of (1.3) will be the same as the maximum value of (1.1), and we can solve for this value at the same time as we solve for the corresponding values of the other unknown variables, the q_{ik}.

The necessary conditions for a maximum value of V require that the partial derivatives of the expression with respect to each of the variables should be equal to zero. We can therefore write n equations, each of the form[5]

$$\frac{\partial V}{\partial q_{ik}} = f_i - \lambda p_i = 0 \qquad (i = 1, \ldots, n) \tag{1.4}$$

and one equation of the form

$$\frac{\partial V}{\partial \lambda} = z_k - \sum_{i=1}^{n} p_i q_{ik} = 0 \tag{1.5}$$

We thus have $(n + 1)$ equations in (1.4) and (1.5) to determine the $(n + 1)$ unknown variables, the $n\, q_{ik}$ and λ. We know that the p_i are given parameters and that the f_i must be functions of q_{ik}, since they are the partial derivatives of function (1.1) above. Since we are not particularly interested in λ, we can use one of our equations to eliminate it.[6] By rearranging terms in the remaining n equations we can express the unknown q_{ik} interms of the parameters p_i and z_k. We thereby obtain n equations, each of the form

$$q_{ik} = g_k(p_1, p_2, \ldots, p_n, z_k) \tag{1.6}$$

These are our demand functions, one for each commodity and each consumer. A simple example of the derivation of such a demand function in the case of two goods is given in chapter 5.

Equations (1.4) and (1.5) state the *necessary* or first-order conditions for a maximum value of utility subject to the budget constraint. Strictly speaking, it is also necessary to ensure that the particular values of the variables satisfy the *sufficient* or second-order conditions for a maximum. Since these are of slight economic significance and algebraically rather complicated, we shall omit any formal statement. Interested readers are referred to Henderson and Quandt (1971) p. 38. Other readers can be assured that the assumptions we have already made guarantee the satisfaction of these conditions.

[5] In the case of a boundary solution, i.e. if $q_{jk} = 0$, then the corresponding equation of set (1.4) may not hold as an equality.

[6] From (1.4) it is clear that $\lambda = f_1/p_1 = f_2/p_2 = \ldots f_n/p_n$. Those who like to think of utility in cardinal terms can identify λ as the marginal utility of the consumer's income.

By reformulating the necessary conditions we can derive another interesting result. From (1.4) it follows that

$$f_i - \lambda p_i = 0 \tag{1.7}$$

and

$$f_j - \lambda p_j = 0 \tag{1.8}$$

Dividing (1.7) by (1.8), we have

$$\frac{f_i}{f_j} = \frac{p_i}{p_j} \tag{1.9}$$

As we have seen, f_i/f_j represents the consumer's subjective rate of substitution in consumption between the pair of goods, i and j. Equation (1.9) tells us that in the consumer's equilibrium the *RSC* will be equal to the price ratio, and that this condition will hold true for all pairs of goods in the consumer's budget. We shall return to this result in our discussion of welfare economics in chapter 9.

In view of the emphasis which demand theory receives in partial equilibrium analysis, we should point out the relationship between a demand function of the form (1.6) and the conventional partial demand function. We have derived (1.6) by treating commodity prices, p_i, and consumer income z, as parameters. But when we include demand functions of the form (1.6) in a complete system of general equilibrium, as we do in chapter 5, then p_i and z are treated as variables. The parameters of the demand function reflect simply the tastes of the consumer. In a conventional demand function, on the other hand, not only are consumer tastes held constant, so also is the consumer's income, and the prices of all commodities except that which is the subject of the study.[7] Thus, in our notation, the partial equilibrium demand function corresponding to (1.6) would be written.

$$q_{ik} = g_k(p_i) \tag{1.10}$$

Two properties of demand functions like (1.6) should be noticed:

(1) The demand for any commodity is a single-valued function of prices and the consumer's income. Our five assumptions were chosen to provide a unique solution, i.e. a single-valued function or

[7] For an alternative formulation of the conventional demand function, see Friedman (1953), pp. 47–99.

set of commodities corresponding to each given set of commodity prices and the consumer's income.

(2) Demand functions are homogeneous of degree zero in prices and consumer's income. This means that if all commodity prices and the consumer income change in proportion, the quantities demanded remain unchanged. This is easily shown:

Suppose all prices and the consumer's income change in the same proportion h. The consumer's budget constraint becomes

$$hz_k - h \sum_{i=1}^{n} p_i q_{ik} = 0 \tag{1.11}$$

$$\therefore \quad h(z_k - \sum_{i=1}^{n} p_i q_{ik}) = 0 \tag{1.12}$$

Since $h \neq 0$, then

$$z_k - \sum_{i=1}^{n} p_i q_{ik} = 0 \tag{1.13}$$

Which is the same as (1.2). Thus the demand function derived from maximising (1.1) subject to (1.11) must be the same as that which was derived from maximising (1.1) subject to (1.2). The property implies consumers do not suffer from "money illusion", and that it is relative commodity prices and not absolute money prices which determine their purchases.

The Supply of Factor Services

Let us suppose that every consumer is endowed with a stock of factor services. The quantity of factor service j held by consumer k can be denoted $\bar{y}_{jk}$, the bar above the variable suggesting that this is a fixed quantity. By selling some or all of his stock of factor services, the consumer earns the income, z_k, which he uses to purchase commodities.

If we assume that the consumer gets utility from retaining some of his stock of factor services (labour services, for example) then it is possible to derive supply functions for factor services from the theory of consumer behaviour in a manner exactly analogous to the derivation of the commodity demand function. Writing the consumer's utility function as

$$u_k = h_k(\bar{y}_{1k} - y_{1k}, \bar{y}_{2k} - y_{2k}, \ldots, \bar{y}_{mk} - y_{mk}) \qquad (1.14)$$

where y_{jk} is the quantity of factor service j supplied by consumer k, this function can be maximised subject to a minimum income constraint. Given their prices, r_j, the quantities of factor services supplied should be such that the consumer's income does not fall below a given amount:

$$z_k = \sum_{i=1}^{m} r_j y_{jk} \qquad (1.15)$$

The resulting factor supply functions then have the form

$$y_{jk} = \phi(r_1, r_2, \ldots, r_m, z_k) \qquad (1.16)$$

Many general equilibrium systems are based upon such functions, but our analysis in later chapters will be greatly facilitated if we assume, instead, that consumers will sell their entire stock of factor services at whatever price prevails. We, in other words, assume perfectly inelastic factor supplies.[8]

Thus our factor supply functions can be written in the simplest form

$$y_{jk} = \bar{y}_{jk} \qquad (1.17)$$

We shall also want to use in our complete system the consumer's budget relation:

$$z_k = \sum_j r_j y_{jk} \qquad (1.18)$$

where r_j denotes the price of factor service j, and z_k the consumer's expenditure.

These relations complete the contribution of the theory of consumer behaviour to our neoclassical general equilibrium system. We turn in the next two chapters to the theory of production.

[8] While it is quite common for this assumption to be made on the grounds of simplifying the exposition, its restrictiveness should not be ignored. In practice, there are very few occasions on which factor services are not responsive to changes in factor prices, yet in empirical analysis this is often overlooked. In our own analysis, the assumption of fixed factor supplies raises the possibility that some households might have zero incomes while continuing to supply factor services.

2 Production Functions

The production function represents the physical transformation possibilities—all the *technically efficient* ways of transforming inputs of factor services into a product. Technically efficient input combinations are those which produce a given output with the minimum physical quantity of each input. Thus if 100 dozen shirts can be produced using 50 square yards of cloth and 20 man-hours of labour, then 50 square yards of cloth and 22 man-hours cannot be a technically efficient way of producing 100 dozen shirts, although 45 square yards of cloth and 22 man-hours may be. Notice that technical efficiency is entirely independent of the prices of the inputs and the product. Thus the neoclassical theory of production can be regarded as a sequence of three processes of optimisation; first, the choice of the technically efficient input combinations; second, the choice of the least cost input combination for each output level; and, finally, the choice of the maximum profit level of output. The specification of a production function presumes that the first optimisation process has already been completed.

Like the utility function in consumer theory, the production function provides the principal parameters for the theory of production, and frequently the algebraic forms in which the two functions are expressed are similar. The analogy is not exact, however. While utility is the maximand in the Theory of Consumption, it is profits, not output, which is the maximand in the Theory of Production. Output is well-defined, cardinal, and empirically measurable, while utility is none of these things. This is why the utility function is not directly included in most general equilibrium analyses while the production function is included.

The properties of any particular system of general equilibrium depend in part upon the properties of the production function which underlies it. We therefore feel it is worthwhile to devote this chapter to a discussion of the properties of different forms of the production function. Many economists have been made aware, by recent controversies, of the significance of the form chosen for the production function in macro-economic growth and distribution theory. Fewer seem to be aware of the extent to which the results of the traditional theory of value, whether stated in partial or general equilibrium terms, depend upon the specific forms chosen for the production function.

Production Functions

Production functions are relations between flows[1] or time rates of input and output in production. In most general form a production function is written

$$x_i = f(y_1, y_2, \ldots, y_m) \tag{2.1}$$

but we can know nothing about the properties of a production function unless these are specified. A classification scheme for specific classes of production function is shown on p. 10; as we travel down the list each forms a sub-class of its predecessor. As we move from the general to the particular, the properties of each class become more restrictively defined. Although we use algebra or graphical methods as a convenient illustration of these properties, we shall really be interested in their economic significance. The two major classes of production function are *Continuous* production functions, which as their name suggests, are attuned to the smooth substitutability requirement of neoclassical theory, and *Linear* production functions, whose simplicity reflects more closely classical economic thinking. For clarity of exposition, we confine ourselves to the two input, one output case, i.e.

$$x = f(y_1, y_2) \tag{2.2}$$

All the properties are general, unless otherwise stated.

[1] An input or output flow is measured in physical units per unit of time, as opposed to a stock which is measured in physical units. Thus one input might be measured in man-hours of a particular type of labour, another might be measured in hours worked by a particular machine, and yet another might be measured in tons of some particular mineral, all offered or demanded within a given time period. If these flows are defined with reference to the single time period within which our analysis takes place, then they can simply be measured in physical units.

Continuous Production Functions

The class of continuous production function can be defined by the four following characteristics:

(i) The function is single valued, everywhere continuous, and well-defined over the range of inputs yielding nonnegative outputs.

(ii) The function has continuous first and second order partial derivatives.

(iii) The inputs are continuously variable.

(iv) Inputs and outputs alike are assumed to be homogeneous, and there is no technical progress.

A very large number of functions may be devised satisfying these conditions. Their properties can be analysed from three standpoints:

(a) The response of output to the variation of a single input, all other inputs being held constant.

(b) The substitution possibilities of one input for another, output being held constant.

(c) The response of output to an equiproportional variation of all inputs.

A Taxonomy of Production Functions

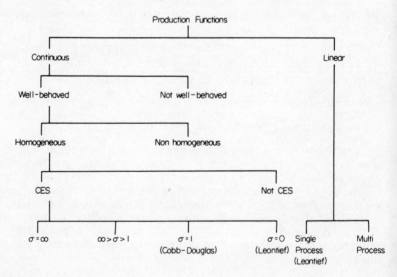

A. *Single Input Variation*

Consider the whole class of continuous production functions from standpoint (a). Three interesting cases can be illustrated diagrammatically. All three cases illustrated in Fig. 2.1 conform to the Law of Variable Proportions, which requires that beyond some point marginal product of an input must be decreasing ($f_{11} < 0$ in our notation). But only case (i) in the diagram conforms to the property

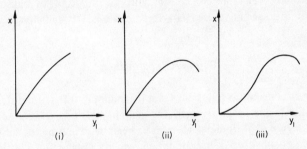

Fig. 2.1   Single input variation in continuous production functions

that marginal product never falls as far as zero ($f_1 > 0$). A little reflection suggests that this is a rather restrictive requirement, but virtually all of the production functions which appear in the literature of neoclassical theory conform to it.[2] They are then said to be "well-behaved" production functions. The class of "well-behaved" production functions can be defined by applying two additional restrictions to those possessed by the general class of continuous functions:

(v) An additive constant term is ruled out, i.e. output cannot be obtained without some input.

(vi) Marginal products must everywhere be positive and decreasing i.e. $f_i > 0, f_{ii} < 0$.

[2] It is true that no combination of inputs in which the marginal product of any input is negative can be technically efficient. Therefore, with positive prices only certain areas of non-"well-behaved" functions could serve as production functions in the sense we have defined them. On the other hand, "well-behaved" functions tend to exaggerate actual substitution possibilities by permitting grossly disproportionate input combinations to be technically efficient.

Following the literature, we shall deal only with those sub-classes of continuous functions which are "well-behaved", such as the CES and Cobb-Douglas forms. It is important however to realise that there are other production functions which may be homogeneous or have constant elasticity of substitution even though not "well-behaved". We might designate those functional forms which correspond to Fig. 2.1(ii) and 2.1(iii) as "acceptable", in the sense that they conform to the Law of Variable Proportions and are empirically just as plausible, if not more so, than their "well-behaved" cousins. But it is important to realise that productions possessing these characteristics are not "well-behaved".

B. *Input Substitution*

Looking at continuous functions from the standpoint (b) of input substitution while output is fixed, the main parameter is the *elasticity of substitution σ*. To understand σ let us begin with another parameter, r, the rate of substitution in production, which can be defined as the rate at which one input is substituted for another in order to leave output unchanged. It is equal to the ratio of the marginal products of the two inputs, f_i/f_j, and of course varies from one point on the production function to another. Writing the ratio of the two inputs as

$$\hat{y} = \frac{y_1}{y_2} \tag{2.3}$$

Then elasticity of substitution is simply defined as

$$\sigma = \frac{d \log \hat{y}}{d \log r} \tag{2.4}$$

i.e. it is the ratio of the proportionate change in the input ratio to the proportionate change in the rate of substitution as output is kept constant. This definition is illustrated in Fig. 2.2. As input 1 is substituted for input 2 one moves along the isoquant $\bar{x}$ from P_1 to P_2. (Strictly speaking these points are so close together as to be in the neighbourhood of a single point.) The change in the input ratio, y, is represented by the change in the angle B, while the change in the rate of substitution, r, is represented by the change in the Angle A. Since the elasticity of substitution is equal to the first divided by the second, it is not difficult to see from the diagram that the flatter is the isoquant

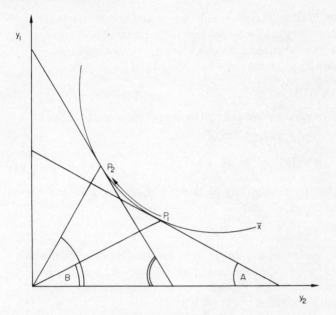

Fig. 2.2   Input substitution

at any given point, the higher will be the value of σ at that point. Thus the value of σ is inversely proportional to the curvature of the isoquant, and varies from 0 to ∞ according to the ease with which one input can be substituted for another. Two other characteristics of σ are worth noting. Like other elasticity parameters, its value is independent of the units in which y_1 and y_2 and x are measured. And the value of σ, which is symmetrical between inputs, in general varies from one point on the isoquant to another. Only a special sub-class of production functions satisfies the restriction that σ is constant at all points on every isoquant; this is the CES (constant elasticity of substitution) class of functions.

C. *Equiproportional Input Variations*

Examined from the standpoint of their response to the variation of a single input, continuous production functions can be divided into two sub-classes: those which are "well-behaved", and those which are not. From the standpoint of input substitution, they can be divided into another two sub-classes—those which have a constant σ and those which do not. Finally, from the standpoint of equiproportional input variation, they can be divided into the sub-class of homogeneous production functions and those which are nonhomogeneous.

Consider any fixed point on a production function,

$$x^0 = f(y_1^0, y_2^0) \tag{2.5}$$

Let each input be changed by the same proportion, λ. Then

$$x = f(\lambda y_1^0, \lambda y_2^0)$$

$$\therefore \qquad \underline{x = f(\lambda)} \tag{2.6}$$

Let us define the elasticity of output with respect to scale as

$$\epsilon = \frac{d \log x}{d \log \lambda} \tag{2.7}$$

If ϵ is constant at all points in a production function, that function is said to be homogeneous. In general, the value of ϵ will vary in a production function, depending on (a) the specific input proportions at x^0, and (b) the level of output at x^0.

If, in the neighbourhood of any point x^0,

$$\epsilon \gtrless 1 \tag{2.8}$$

then we say that the function is respectively subject to increasing, constant or decreasing returns to scale at that point. A production function which exhibits different classes of returns to scale at different levels of output is clearly nonhomogeneous, even though this might be thought to be quite a plausible, even normal, phenomenon.

Homogeneous Production Functions

When

$$x = f(y_1, y_2, \ldots, y_m) \tag{2.9}$$

Then a production function is said to be homogeneous of degree s if

$$\lambda^s x = f(\lambda y_1, \lambda y_2, \ldots, \lambda y_m) \tag{2.10}$$

and exhibits increasing, constant or decreasing returns to scale respectively, *throughout*, according as

$$s \gtrless 1 \tag{2.11}$$

While production functions homogeneous of degree one[3] are very common in the literature of economic theory, those having $s > 1$ are rare. The popularity of production functions homogeneous of degree one is not accidental: it is explained by an extremely significant property of homogeneous functions, viz. that they all satisfy the following identity:

$$y_1 f_1 + y_2 f_2 \equiv sx \qquad\qquad (2.12)$$

This identity may be given the following economic interpretation. Suppose that the total output, x is distributed among the owners of inputs (y_j) according to the principle that each input receives its *physical* marginal product (f_j) per unit of input, then if

    $s > 1$, the total dividend will exceed the total product
    $s < 1$, the total dividend will be less than the total product
    $s = 1$, the total dividend will exactly exhaust the total product

Thus, while the cases of $s \gtrless 1$ might appear to pose difficulties for a theory of distribution based on the marginal productivity principle, the production function homogeneous of degree one, which provides for exact exhaustion of the product, is apparently congenial to neoclassical theory.[4]

Two other properties of homogeneous functions are of particular significance for neoclassical theory. The first is that the first-order partial derivatives of a function homogeneous of degree s are themselves homogeneous of degree $(s - 1)$. This means that the marginal products of constant returns to scale production functions are constant with respect to scale of output. Secondly, the expansion path (i.e. the locus of points on each isoquant representing a constant value of the rate of input substitution, r) of all homogeneous functions is a straight line through the origin.[5]

  [3] Such functions are sometimes known in the literature as "linear homogeneous", which is a source of unnecessary confusion. They have nothing to do with linear production functions.

  [4] The matter is not quite so simple as this account suggests. See p. 23 below.

  [5] But not all linear expansion paths belong to homogeneous production functions.

The CES Production Function

We come now to a form of production function whose use in the literature has grown rapidly since it was first proposed some ten years ago.[6] It is that sub-class of homogeneous of degree one production functions which have a constant elasticity of substitution.[7]

The algebraic form of this type of function in the two input case is the rather ungainly expression

$$x = \gamma [\beta y_1^{-\rho} + (1 - \beta) y_2^{-\rho}]^{-1/\rho} \tag{2.13}$$

There are three parameters:

γ the *efficiency* parameter, which acts as a simple multiplicative factor. $\gamma > 0$

β the *input intensity* parameter. The greater is β, the greater is the y_1/y_2 ratio and thus the y_1 intensity of the productive process. $0 < \beta < 1$

ρ the *substitution* parameter. This is simply another form of the elasticity of substitution since $\rho = 1/\sigma - 1$. Since $\sigma \geqslant 0$, then it follows $\infty \geqslant \rho \geqslant -1$

Four particular cases are of some interest, each corresponding to a specific value for the substitution parameter.

(i) $\sigma = \infty, \rho = -1$

In this case, there is perfect substitutability between the two inputs. The isoquants of the function are parallel straight lines (see Fig. 2.3(i)).

(ii) $\sigma = k, k \neq 0, 1 \text{ or } \infty$

This is the general case, covering all values of other than ∞, 0, or 1. There is a slight difference in this case, according to whether $\sigma \gtrless 1$.

---

[6] Arrow, Chenery, Minhas, and Solow (1961).

[7] Not only are there functions homogeneous of degree one which have variable elasticities of substitution, but there are also constant elasticity of substitution functions which are not homogeneous of degree one (e.g. $x = y_1^{\alpha} y_2^{\beta}$, where $\alpha + \beta \neq 1$), and therefore do *not* belong to the CES class we are discussing.

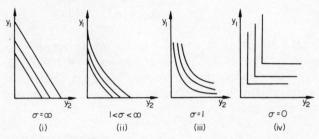

Fig. 2.3   Isoquants of the CES production function for different values of σ.

When $\sigma > 1$ (i.e. $-1 < \rho < 0$), the marginal product approaches asymptotically a positive finite limit, i.e. the isoquants cut both axes.

When $\sigma < 1$ (i.e. $\rho > 0$), the marginal product approaches zero asymptotically, i.e. the isoquants are asymptotic to lines parallel to the axes.

$$\text{(iii)} \quad \sigma = 1, \rho = 0$$

Strictly speaking we should write $\sigma \to 1$, for the form (2.13) is not defined for $\rho = 0$. As $\sigma \to 1$ the form becomes the familiar Cobb–Douglas expression

$$x = y_1^{\alpha} y_2^{\beta} \tag{2.14}$$

and the isoquants are asymptotic to the axes.

It will be recalled that when $\alpha + \beta = 1$, the Cobb–Douglas is homogeneous of degree one. It is essential *not* to confuse this property with the substitution parameter, $\sigma = 1$. The distinction can be clarified by pointing out that in the *general* case of the Cobb–Douglas (*not* the one familiar in the literature), where $\alpha + \beta \neq 1$, then we have a production function where elasticity of substitution is constant and equal to one, but which is homogeneous of degree other than one.

Now, the "traditional" ($\alpha + \beta = 1$) version of the Cobb–Douglas production function widely used in the literature before the advent of the more general CES form, has the following properties: it (a) is "well-behaved", (b) has $\sigma = 1$ everywhere, and (c) is homogeneous of degree one. These properties can easily be proved. From what has been said so far in this chapter, it should be clear that they are based on highly restrictive assumptions. As shown in Fig. 2.3(iii), the isoquants of this form are asymptotic to the axes.

$$(iv) \ \sigma = 0, \rho = \infty$$

This is again a limiting case, where we should strictly write $\sigma \to 0$, since the standard CES form (2.13) is not defined for $\rho = \infty$. Instead, the case of a production function homogeneous of degree one, for which σ is everywhere constant but zero is represented by a linear function of the Leontief type, written

$$x \leq \frac{1}{a_1} y_1 \tag{2.15}$$

$$x \leq \frac{1}{a_2} y_2 \tag{2.16}$$

The isoquants of this function are L shaped, as illustrated in Fig. 2.3(iv). Marginal products are either positive and constant or zero, depending upon the particular point on the function and upon which input is varied.

As the value of $\sigma = 0$ implies, there is no possibility of input substitution. This limiting case is therefore not a continuous function at all but is one of the class of linear production functions.

Linear Production Functions

While continuous functions permit variable input proportions, linear functions are characterised by fixed input combinations. Despite their formal dissimilarities the two families of functions are, in fact, closely related as we have just seen.

Formally, linear production functions represent production relations as a set of equations, linear in form, with one equation normally for each input. Generally, the relations are represented by inequalities, since only points like A and B in Fig. 2.4(i) satisfy the strict equality.

A. *Single Input Variation in Linear Functions*

Marginal products are generally not uniquely defined. As may be seen from Fig. 2.4(i), they may be either positive or zero depending where on the function one is, and depending whether the input change is an increase or decrease. Taking the partial derivative of a linear function yields constant terms, so the functions are not "well-behaved" in the sense defined earlier.

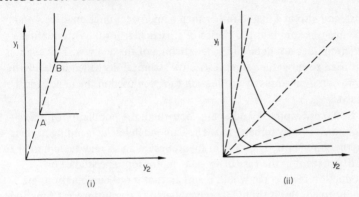

Fig. 2.4   Linear production functions

B. *Input Substitution*

While there is no direct substitution between inputs, the possibility
exists in some linear production functions of substitution between
fixed combinations of inputs (known as processes or activities). As the
number of processes is increased (Fig. 2.4(ii)), a continuous production
function provides the limiting case of the multiprocess linear
production function. The multiprocess function illustrates clearly that
while such "continuous" concepts as the rate of substitution, r, remain
formally undefined in linear functions, and while marginal rules do not
hold, analogies do exist. The equivalence between continuous and linear
concepts is demonstrated more fully in chapter 14.

C. *Equiproportional Input Variation*

In the single process case linear production functions generally exhibit
constant returns to scale, although not necessarily in the multiprocess
case.

Concluding Remarks on Production Functions

In a purely theoretical analysis, the choice of production function
depends upon the purpose and context of the analysis. One would
expect that substitution possibilities would be greater *ex ante* than *ex*

post, and also in a macro rather than a microeconomic analysis.[8] But one must beware that the choice of a particular form of production function does not determine the outcome of the analysis. This chapter has tried to show the rather restrictive assumptions which underlie the more common forms of production function used in the neoclassical analysis.

So far as empirical studies are concerned, the popularity of linear functions is easily understood. They are much less demanding in their data requirements. Their use in theoretical analysis may seem harder to justify; except in the case of *ex post* microeconomic studies of production few people would maintain that input combinations are rigidly fixed. But it should be remembered that multiprocess functions do allow for substitution between groups of inputs, and thus may be empirically more plausible than models of continuously variable inputs. And the single fixed input combinations may be regarded as a reasonable approximation to the actual production possibilities, where the range of input substitution is restricted.

[8] The problems encountered in aggregating inputs place severe limitations on the usefulness of an aggregate production function. See Robinson (1953).

3 Theory of Production

Neoclassical economic theory has been described[1] as a system bred by philosophical utilitarianism out of the differential calculus. It will not be surprising, therefore, to discover the methodological similarities between the Theory of Production and the Theory of Consumption. In chapter 1, we derived two sets of relationships from the theory of consumption. These were (1) equilibrium conditions for consumers, and (2) demand functions for consumer goods. In this chapter we shall derive two further components of our neoclassical general equilibrium system, (3) a set of equilibrium conditions for producers, and (4) a set of demand functions for inputs of factor services. We shall derive these from the Theory of Production. In that Theory we assume that the unit of production, the firm, produces a single commodity using inputs of two or more factor services. We assume further that it is too small to influence *either* the price it receives for its product *or* the prices it pays for the inputs it purchases. Thus from the point of view of the firm, the prices of the inputs and the output are parameters and the level of output is the unknown variable whose value is to be determined. But from the point of view of the economy as a whole, prices as well as output levels are unknown variables. The behavioural assumption in production theory which corresponds to utility maximisation in consumer theory is that the firm arranges its level of output and purchases of inputs in such a way as to maximise profits.

Consider a firm, f, which produces a single commodity, x_i^f, using several inputs, each denoted y_{ji}^f. Then the profits of the firm can be written as total revenue less total costs:

$$\pi = p_i x_i^f - c \tag{3.1}$$

[1] Walsh (1970).

The firm's production function can then be written as

$$x_i^f = \phi(y_{1i}^f, y_{2i}^f, \ldots, y_{mi}^f) \tag{3.2}$$

Now costs, c, can be divided into the costs of the variable inputs

$$\sum_{j=1}^{m} r_j y_{ji}^f,$$

plus perhaps some element of fixed cost, b, so that (3.1) can be rewritten as:

$$\pi = p_i \phi(y_{1i}^f, y_{2i}^f, \ldots, y_{mi}^f) - \sum_{j=1}^{m} r_j y_{ji}^f - b \tag{3.3}$$

The problem for the firm is to choose that level of output and the associated combination of inputs which will make its profits as large as possible. For maximum values of the expression (3.3), the partial derivatives of π with respect to each of the y_{ji}^f must be equal to zero, i.e.

$$\frac{\partial \pi}{\partial y_{ji}^f} = p_i \phi_j - r_j = 0 \qquad \text{for} \qquad j = 1, 2, \ldots, m \tag{3.4}$$

$$\therefore \qquad r_j = p_i \phi_j \tag{3.5}$$

Unlike the partial derivatives of the utility function which were encountered in chapter one, the partial derivatives of the production function, the ϕ_j, are measurable magnitudes. They represent the marginal products of the relevant inputs. Therefore, (3.5) states the equality of the price of each input with its marginal revenue product. This is a necessary condition for maximum profit. Sufficient conditions for maximum profit under our assumptions require that the marginal product of each input should be decreasing at the point where the necessary conditions are satisfied.[2]

In constructing our general equilibrium system we are less interested in the necessary conditions for a profit maximum than we are in the demand functions for the inputs of factor services which can be derived from them. We have in (3.4) m equations. The variables are the input prices r_j, and the single product price p_i. The ϕ_j are the partial derivatives, with respect to the corresponding input y_j^f, of the production function. They are therefore expressions in terms of y_j^f.

[2] See Henderson and Quandt (1971) p. 68.

Accordingly, we can rearrange the terms in the set of equations (3.4) so as to express the unknown y_j^f in terms of their prices and the single product price:

$$y_{ji}^f = y_{ji}^f(p_i, r_1, r_2, \ldots, r_m) \qquad j = 1, \ldots, m \tag{3.6}$$

The precise functional form of the equations in (3.6) as in (3.4) will depend on the specific form which is assigned to the production function (3.2). These are our input demand functions, one for each firm, each input and each product. The input demand function is homogeneous of degree zero in these prices.

By a simple re-arrangement of (3.5), we have

$$\frac{r_j}{\phi_j} = p_i \tag{3.7}$$

i.e. marginal cost = price. This is the familiar *short-run* equilibrium condition for the firm which, like the input demand functions, derives from the first-order conditions for profit maximisation. It is called short-run, because the profits realised according to (3.4) may be positive, zero, or negative, whereas in the long-run maximum profits must be zero. Otherwise, a surplus or deficit would remain unexplained in the sense that it could not be imputed to any input. To say that maximum profits must be zero is the same as saying that a firm's total costs must equal its total revenue, *or* that its average cost must equal its price. All three statements are equivalent. We shall require our general equilibrium system to satisfy both the short-run (price equals marginal cost) and the long-run (price equals average cost) equilibrium conditions.[3]

In the last chapter we showed how a production function homogeneous of degree one had the apparently convenient property that if each input were paid its marginal product, the total physical product would be exactly exhausted. Such a production function would therefore appear to be highly appropriate for our purposes. It is however too much of a good thing. For, with constant returns to scale

---

[3] Zero long run profits and nonzero short-run profits are usually reconciled by the conceptual device of allowing firms to move costlessly between industries (i.e. from the production of one commodity to another). This, however, raises the possibility of discontinuities in input demand functions which makes it impossible to prove general existence-of-equilibrium theorems, (see chapter 6).

throughout, and prices treated as parameters, average revenue, average cost and therefore profit per unit of output are constant throughout. From the point of view of profit maximisation, there are only three possibilities. If prices are such that profit per unit is positive, maximum total profit will be realised by an unlimited level of output. If, on the other hand, unit profit is negative it will be most profitable not to produce at all. Finally, if unit profit is zero, any level of output will realise the same total profit—zero. Thus the use of a production function homogeneous of degree one leads to a conclusion in which the size of the firm is indeterminate.

However, if

(a) the production function is *not* homogeneous of degree one, and
(b) the first and second order conditions for profit maximisation are satisfied with respect to all the factors of production, and
(c) the firm's total cost is equal to its total revenue then this would represent a position of both short-run and long-run equilibrium.

The satisfaction of condition (b) is implicit in our input demand equations. In order for our general equilibrium system to satisfy (c), this condition must be spelled out explicitly, in one of the three alternative forms. If we choose to write it in the form that the firm's total revenue should equal costs, this will be

$$p_i x_i^f = \sum_{j=1}^{m} r_j y_{ji}^f \qquad (3.8)$$

If the form of our unspecified production function satisfies condition (a) then the size of the firm will be determined. If not, it will remain undetermined, as therefore will the number of firms.

Some Remarks on the Profit Maximisation Hypothesis

Since the central behavioural assumption of the neoclassical theory of production—the profit maximisation hypothesis—has been the subject of some misunderstanding, a few remarks justifying its use in the present context are in order. The key phrase is "in the present context", for the first point which needs to be made—and it is a perfectly general one—is that the choice of ingredients for any theory depend very largely on the uses to which that theory is to be put. The example quoted in the Introduction concerning the ordnance survey map and the church guide book is appropriate in this connection.

If one were engaged upon a detailed analysis of the behaviour of a single firm or a group of firms within one industry, it might be naive indeed to use the hypothesis of profit maximisation as a predictive device. This hypothesis would be even less appropriate if one were concerned with the internal organisation of the firm. More complicated alternatives are available which would almost certainly be more fruitful in that context.

However, if one is concerned with the analysis of a complete economic system, composed of thousands, if not hundreds of thousands of firms, operating in various industries under widely differing conditions, then it is difficult to think of a unifying behavioural assumption which is as general or as simple as that of profit maximisation. Where alternative hypotheses have been proposed, e.g. the maximisation of the growth rate of the present value of the firm's assets, they do not appear to predict differently the signs of the relevant partial derivatives. This means, for example, that under both hypotheses a rise in an input price will be expected to diminish the demand for that input, and a rise in the output price to increase it.

Most of the controversy has concerned the role of the profit maximisation hypothesis as a predictive device. But, as we shall see in our discussion of welfare economics in chapter 9, it plays an important part in normative analysis as well. This is because many of the equilibrium conditions associated with profit maximisation turn out to have properties related to allocative efficiency. It may be argued that in a decentralised but efficient economic system—whether capitalist or socialist—firms *ought* to be trying to maximise their profits, even if they don't.

4 Theory of Markets

The Market Mechanism and Economic Organisation

In our discussion so far, we have assumed that prices were given to consumers and to producers. Such an assumption corresponds equally to a perfectly competitive market economy and a centrally planned economy. Now that we are turning in this chapter to a consideration of how prices are determined, we must recognise that methods of price determination will vary according to the prevailing form of economic organisation.

In market economies, there is not one form of organisation, but several, ranging from perfect competition to pure monopoly. Most students will already be familiar with models of imperfect competition in market economies, and their relation to general equilibrium analysis is discussed in the following section. In centrally planned economies one might propose three models of organisation. There is first of all the pure command economy, in which every single decision in the whole economy is centrally determined. In this case, there is no need for an allocative mechanism, since the decisions may be supposed to be handed down for implementation by *fiat*. There need therefore be no explicit price system.[1] Computation of a set of decisions which were consistent, however, would seem to depend on the existence of some form of general equilibrium model. At the opposite extreme in a centrally-planned economy, there is the possibility of simulating the organisation of a competitive market economy, in the manner suggested by Lange (1937), Lerner (1937), Sik (1967) and others. Such a model does not differ in any essential respect from the perfect competition model of a market economy: in the case of the centrally planned economy, pro-

---

[1] However, a price system would be implicit in the allocation, as is shown in chapter 9.

ducers are not entrepreneurs but managers of state-owned firms. Then there is an intermediate model which perhaps corresponds most closely to the organisation of real-world centrally planned economies. According to this model, which is due to Mirrlees (1969), households purchase consumer goods and offer labour services, without restriction, at prevailing prices. Producers, on the other hand, are strictly controlled by the government, which lays down rules for their behaviour. The nature of the rules determines the extent to which decision making in the sphere of production may be decentralised. If, for example, (1) producers are prevented from exercising monopolistic influences, and (2) prices are such as to equate supply and demand, and (3) producers are instructed to maximise profits measured at such prices, then considerable decentralisation will result. Such a decentralised system will have two major advantages over a completely centralised or command economy. First, there is a significant advantage in the handling of information. The information which each producer requires about the rest of the economy is summarised in the market prices of inputs and outputs. This information can then be combined with the producer's own special information about his particular production possibilities. It would be very difficult to centralise the latter type of information. Secondly, the decentralisation of decision making according to the foregoing rules is self-regulating, and should eliminate the need for that detailed checking to ensure that instructions have been carried out which is implicit in a centralised system. Two criticisms however, can be directed against the decentralised system. First, that it makes it difficult, although not impossible, for there to be any precise control over the distribution of income. Secondly, many current production decisions depend not on current prices, but on expectations of prices yet to be determined, and it is argued that a decentralised system does not predict prices well. In this view, central planning and a market mechanism are complementary rather than competing forms of organisation. While the market can determine current prices more effectively, the prediction of prices (i.e. the formation of price-expectations) would be the role of a central authority.[2]

[2] It should be emphasised that this is simply one point of view. Whether, in practice, a central authority would prove to be a more accurate predictor of prices than a market mechanism remains to be tested. What may be more readily accepted is the proposition that uncertainty about the future creates a greater risk for the decentralised than for the centralised decision maker, and that therefore investment may take place at a lower rate under the former type of régime.

Imperfect Markets and General Equilibrium

Three fundamental forms of organisation can be distinguished in a market economy. There is first of all general monopolistic competition, including the case of pure monopoly; secondly, there is oligopoly, and then there is perfect competition. The case of monopolistic competition can be distinguished from oligopoly in that an "average revenue" function, in which the quantity of output sold by the monopolistic producer is expressed as a function of its own price, can be said to exist for the former, but not for the latter. However, in the case of monopolistic competition the curve corresponding to this function is downward-sloping, rather than horizontal as it is in the case of perfect competition.

In our model of neoclassical general equilibrium, we confine ourselves exclusively to the case in which prices are given to all producers and consumers, i.e. to perfect competition in the context of a market economy or to a decentralised system in the context of a planned economy. Why do we do this?

The omission of monopolistic competition may be justified on the grounds of simplicity: to introduce the necessary assumptions to give effect to this form would complicate our analysis inordinately. And it may be argued that the case of a large group of firms producing differentiated products is not very different in its long-run equilibrium from that of perfect competition.[3] And we know that a solution for a general equilibrium in the case of monopolistic competition can be proved to exist.[4]

By contrast, there seems no way in which oligopoly can be satis-factorily included in a neoclassical general equilibrium analysis. The existence of an "average revenue" curve depends upon a producer being able to determine the effect of changes in the price of his own product upon its own sales. But this cannot be done if sales depend upon the reactions of an oligopolistic rival which may be unforseeable or unpredictable. Of course, it is quite possible that in a specific situation these reactions, either because of collusion or from observation of past behaviour, may conform to a predictable pattern. But there are a large number of possible reaction patterns, sketched in various theories of

---

[3] Monopolistic profits attract new entrants and/or the innovation of substitute products, making short-term profits difficult to sustain in the long-run.

[4] See Arrow and Hahn (1971), and Negishi (1961).

oligopoly behaviour, and few would argue that any one of them should be generalised. If they were, and oligopolistic interdependence were to be included within a neoclassical system, then it seems likely that the existence and stability of a general equilibrium solution would be threatened. In view of the prevalence of oligopoly as an organisational form in contemporary market economies, the inability of the neoclassical analysis to cope with oligopoly must be regarded as a serious deficiency.[5]

Conditions for a Perfect Market

A perfect market can be defined by four conditions or assumptions:

(i) *Product homogeneity.* This rules out product differentiation. It says that consumers have no reason to prefer goods produced by one firm to the same[6] goods produced by another. It also rules out producer discrimination including such practices as selling an amount of goods on the basis of "first come, first served".

(ii) *The alteration of quantities of goods produced by an individual firm or consumed by an individual household has no effect on the price of those goods.* This implies that sales by each firm and purchases by each household are very small in relation to the aggregate volume of transactions. In partial equilibrium terms, each firm is assumed to face a horizontal demand curve for its product, and each household a horizontal supply curve for its individual purchases of any commodity.

(iii) *Perfect information* about prevailing prices and bids (see below) is presumed to exist on both sides of the market. Taken together with (i) and the assumption of utility maximisation, this condition suffices to ensure that a single price for any goods prevails in a perfect market.

[5] The consequences may be more serious for the analysis than for the real world. Their performance does not suggest that the price behaviour of oligopolies has a destabilising effect on markets in general, rather their effect is to distort the transmission of price information from one sector to another. If the neoclassical system is regarded as a normative rather than a predictive model than it may be argued that the deficiency lies with market economies in permitting the existence of oligopolistic behaviour.

[6] Sameness refers to the economic not the physical characteristics of goods. If two goods are physically identical, but one is preferred by some consumers, they should be treated as two different goods.

(iv) *Free entry to and exit from a market* for both producers and consumers. This ensures a costless flow of inputs between industries.

Market Demand and Supply–Commodities

We are familiar, from partial equilibrium analysis, with the concepts of market demand and supply. These concepts also play their part in general equilibrium analysis, although in slightly different form since we are dealing not just with a single market, but with equilibrium in a whole set of markets simultaneously. Recall that we derived the demand function of the individual household k for good i in the form (1.6):

$$q_{ik} = g(p_1, p_2, \ldots, p_n, z_k) \tag{4.1}$$

This means that the quantity demanded is a function of the whole set of prices and the income of the household. If our general equilibrium system is to be able to take account of the effect of changes in the distribution of income among households upon the demand for commodities, then we must leave equations like (4.1) disaggregated.

If we include a set of input demand functions within our system, then we can dispense with a set of supply functions for commodities, since both are derived from the same parameters and behavioural assumptions. If we can dispense with commodity supply functions, then we can dispense with cost functions also. In this way we can short cut the traditional path taken by partial equilibrium analysis, going first from the production function to cost functions then to the supply function.

Market Demand and Supply–Factors

The demand functions for inputs of factor services were derived in the last chapter directly from the theory of the firm. We can include these functions in our general equilibrium system without further modification.

On p. 7, we indicated how supply functions for factor services might be derived from the theory of consumption. But we also pointed out there that, for simplicity, we would assume perfectly inelastic supplies of all factors: (1.17):

$$y_{jk} = \bar{y}_{jk}$$

Taken in conjunction with the consumer's income relationship (1.18):

$$z_k = \sum_j r_j y_{jk}$$

this implies a prior distribution of supplies of factor services among households. Once the prices of factors are determined in the solution to the system then of course the income distribution is determined. If this income distribution is unacceptable, then it may be changed by either (a) redistributing the original supplies of factor services, *or* (b) adding an equation to redistribute the incomes between households.

A more general system than the one we describe here would of course be formulated if we specified input supply functions. Then the consequences of income redistributive measures would be considerably more complicated, but probably more realistic.[7]

---

[7] A misplaced criticism of the neoclassical general equilibrium analysis which is sometimes heard is that it attempts to "justify" the set of market-determined prices actually prevailing, yet such prices are not independent of the current distribution of income. This line of argument is thoroughly confused. First of all, the analysis is entirely independent of any particular set of prices, as may be seen by substituting for (1.18) the relationship

$$z_k = t_k \left(\sum_k \sum_j r_j y_{jk} \right)$$

where

$$\sum_{k=1}^{s} t_k = 1$$

and allowing the values of t_k to vary from one experiment to another. For any set of t, i.e. for any specified distribution of income between households, there would be a different set of equilibrium prices. Indeed, as the next chapter makes clear, a change in one parameter could be expected to change the value of all the unknown variables in the system. It is only by means of a neoclassical general equilibrium analysis that the interdependence of prices, output levels, income distribution and all the other parameters and variables in the economic system is made explicit. In a fully-developed analysis, with input supply functions, a redistribution of income would be revealed to alter not only the set of prices, but also the supply of factor services, a phenomenon which is frequently overlooked in practice.

Market Equilibrium

The meaning and significance of market equilibrium is discussed in some detail in chapter 6. For the moment we will content ourselves with a sketch of how, in the neoclassical view, an equilibrium is reached. Until quite recently this process might have seemed self-evident, but a renewed interest in the analysis of disequilibrium,[8] has led to the logic of the process being questioned. It therefore seems to be worth mentioning.

Starting off with an initial bid at some arbitrary price, the ultimate market equilibrium is envisaged as being reached by a process of recontracting, according to which a buyer and seller who enter a contract reserve the right to re-contract with anyone who makes a more favourable offer. An imaginary "auctioneer" records all bids, and bidding only ceases when no-one has any motive to change the bids. This will happen only when there are no unsatisfied buyers or sellers, i.e. when the equilibrium price-quantity combination has been established. Thus no transactions take place except at the equilibrium price.

From the point of view of our analysis the market equilibrium condition may be stated *either* as "supply price equals demand price" *or* as "quantity supplied equals quantity demanded". The latter statement expresses the condition in terms of variables which appear elsewhere in the system, so we choose it.

The equilibrium condition (or market clearing equation) for the market in any good i can then be simply written as:

$$\sum_{k=1}^{s} q_{ik} = \sum_{f=1}^{F} x_i^f \qquad (i = 1, \ldots, n) \tag{4.2}$$

i.e. the aggregate of all the amounts of good i demanded by each household must exactly equal the aggregate of all the amounts of the same good produced by each firm engaged in its production.

Likewise, the equilibrium condition for the market in any factor j can be written as:

$$\sum_{f=1}^{F} \sum_{i=1}^{n} y_{ji}^f = \sum_{k=1}^{s} \bar{y}_{jk} \qquad (j = 1, \ldots, m) \tag{4.3}$$

[8] See, for example, the contributions of Clower (1965) and Leijonhufvud (1968), discussed by Hines (1971).

i.e. the sum of all inputs of type j used by all firms in the production of all goods must be exactly equal to the total amount of that input supplied by each household.

Conclusion

We have now set out all the ingredients for our neoclassical general equilibrium system. In the next chapter we shall put them together and discuss the uses and limitations of the resulting system.

PART II
Neoclassical General Equilibrium Analysis

5 A Neoclassical System of General Equilibrium

In this chapter we present a neoclassical general equilibrium system, followed by a two sector numerical example.

Our system, only one of many of the neoclassical type, is composed of six sets of equations, all of them previously derived in chapters 1, 3 or 4.

Demand Equations for Consumer Goods

$$q_{ik} = g_k(p_1, p_2, \ldots, p_n, z_k) \qquad \begin{aligned} i &= 1, \ldots, n \\ k &= 1, \ldots, s \end{aligned} \tag{5.1}$$

Equilibrium Conditions for Consumers

$$z_k = \sum_j r_j \bar{y}_{jk} \qquad \begin{aligned} j &= 1, \ldots, m \\ k &= 1, \ldots, s \end{aligned} \tag{5.2}$$

Demand Equations for Inputs of Factor Services

$$y_{ji}^f = y_{ji}^f(p_i, r_1, r_2, \ldots, r_m) \qquad \begin{aligned} i &= 1, \ldots, n \\ j &= 1, \ldots, m \\ f &= 1, \ldots, F \end{aligned} \tag{5.3}$$

Production Equilibrium Conditions

$$p_i x_i^f = \sum_{j=1}^m r_j y_{ji}^f \qquad \begin{aligned} i &= 1, \ldots, n \\ j &= 1, \ldots, m \\ f &= 1, \ldots, F \end{aligned} \tag{5.4}$$

Commodity Market Clearing Equations

$$\sum_{k=1}^{s} q_{ik} = \sum_{f=1}^{F} x_i^f \qquad i = 1, \ldots, n \qquad (5.5)$$

Factor Market Clearing Equations

$$\sum_{f=1}^{F} \sum_{i=1}^{n} y_{ji}^f = \sum_{k=1}^{s} \bar{y}_{jk} \qquad j = 1, \ldots, m \qquad (5.6)$$

To check that this system of equations may, in fact, have a solution we can first of all compare the total number of equations with the number of unknown variables.

Equation set	Unknown variables in set	Number of variables	Number of equations
(5.1)	q_{ik}	ns	ns
(5.2)	z_k	s	s
(5.3)	y_{ji}^f	nmF	nmF
(5.4)	x_i^f	nF	nF
(5.5)	p_i	n	n
(5.6)	r_j	m	m
Totals		N	N

Thus, there are ns equations in the first set, since there is a demand equation for each commodity by each household. But there is also the same number of the variables q_{ik}, the unkown amounts of each commodity i consumed by each household k. Notice that there are some other unknown variables in (5.1), viz. the z_k, so that we cannot solve (5.1) independently of the rest of the system. The listing of unknown variables in each set in the foregoing table is simply designed to facilitate the counting of equations and variables. It is easy to see, by this method, that there are exactly the same number of equations in total as there are unknown variables, N.[1]

Unfortunately, as we shall see when we discuss questions concerning

---

[1] $N = n [1 + F (1 + m) + s] + s + m.$

the existence of solutions in the following chapter, this fact alone does not guarantee that there is a solution to our system. But we can take some comfort from knowing that if we had found that the number of equations did differ from the number of unknowns, then we should almost certainly not have been able to get a solution.

There is one important complication which we must immediately take into account. If we aggregate the household budget constraints (5.2) over all households, and recall that in our system all household income is spent on consumption, we shall have arrived at the familiar national income accounting identity between factor incomes and expenditure on goods. Thus in systems of our type, under any set of prices, the aggregate value of goods supplied on the market must equal the aggregate value demanded. If supply equals demand on $(n - 1)$ markets, as we require it to do in our market-clearing equations, then the equality must automatically hold on the nth market, too. Our market-clearing equation for that market is then superfluous. To explain this more generally, if we have N equations in our system, then we have only $(N - 1)$ *independent* equations. This means that we can only hope to solve for $(N - 1)$ variables. But, as we have seen, we have N unknown variables. We must therefore eliminate one if we are to have a chance of getting a solution.

Suppose we decide to eliminate one of the price variables by giving it an arbitrary value, and expressing all the other price variables as ratios of that price. Then we shall obtain a solution.[2] But in this solution, the values we obtain for all but one of the price variables will be relative to the value assigned arbitrarily to the one chosen as numéraire. If all the prices obtained in this solution are multiplied by some common (arbitrary) constant, then all the equations of the system will still hold, and the values for the quantities of inputs and outputs will remain unchanged. This means that we can solve a system like ours for *relative* prices only. On reflection we can see that it would be surprising if it were otherwise. We should scarcely expect to be able to solve for the *absolute* value of prices when the monetary factors which determine the level, as opposed to the ratio, of prices do not enter our system.

So much for the preliminary technicalities. Suppose that we know that a solution to our system exists, what will it mean? It can best be regarded as a highly simplified model of the working of a complete decentralised economic system. It shows how, given certain parameters

---

[2] Subject of course to all the qualifications discussed in chapter 6.

and assumptions, the prices (p_i) and quantities (x_i), of all goods produced in the system are determined, as well as the distribution of these goods among households, (q_{ik}). It also shows the prices determined for inputs (r_j), their use in the process of production (y^f_{ji}), and the resulting incomes of households, (z_k). The number of goods, inputs, and households is, in principle, unlimited.

The simplification comes in the implicit assumption that all the significant aspects of a decentralised system, (significant that is from the viewpoint of price-quantity determination, the theory of value), have been included in the relationships specified in our system. We consider below some of the more important influences which have been left out. But let us first look at the factors which, according to a neoclassical system, determine the nature of the solution.

The equilibrium set of prices and quantities depends upon the technology, preferences and resources of the system as well as upon the underlying behavioural, institutional, and technological assumptions. We shall show in Part III that other general equilibrium systems can be constructed based upon quite different assumptions. It is sufficient to emphasise here that under a neoclassical system such as this each decision-making unit operates independently, and treats prices as data. Every household acts as if it were trying to maximise its utility, and each firm acts as if it were trying to maximise its profits. The outcome is a unique solution for relative prices and absolute quantities of inputs and outputs, such that each output is produced and sold at its lowest unit cost in the quantity desired by each household. All markets are cleared. And all markets are interdependent: the simultaneous solution of the system implies that the price of any one good will be affected by a change in the price of any other. Finally, the system is homogeneous of degree zero in absolute prices: if the values of all the price variables are increased equiproportionately, the values of the quantity variables will be left unchanged.

These properties are characteristic not just of the foregoing system but of all general equilibrium systems which describe themselves as neoclassical. Contemporary neoclassical theory as exemplified in the works of Debreu (1959) and of Arrow (1968) may be seen as the refinement of an intellectual tradition stretching back from Walras to Smith via Menger. This tradition has sought to show, in the words of Arrow and Hahn, "that a decentralised economy motivated by self-interest and guided by price signals would be compatible with a coherent disposition of economic resources that could be regarded in a well-defined sense as superior to a large class of possible alternative dispositions".[3]

Criticisms of Neoclassical General Equilibrium Analysis

The neoclassical analysis has been severely criticised, and it will be sufficient here to outline the major lines of criticism. In considering these criticisms, the question to be borne in mind is not "Is the neoclassical system true?" because a theory can never be "true" in the literal sense, but rather the appropriate question is "could it be true?". If one decides the answer to the second question is "no", then one is either accepting that the relative prices and quantities of goods produced in real-world economies are established by the outcome of random or anarchic processes, or else one has in mind some alternative theory of value.

A. *Existence, Uniqueness and Stability of Solutions*

The first set of major criticisms of the neoclassical system contains arguments such as the following. While a system such as the one outlined above may very well have a solution, we have not demonstrated that there are sufficient conditions for a solution always to exist. Nor have we shown that there will only be a single solution and not many possible sets of prices and quantities satisfying the conditions specified. Nor that a small change in one of the variables may not lead to clearly unacceptable values for some of the others. Such questions concerning the existence, uniqueness, and stability properties of solutions to a system are discussed in the following chapter. Meanwhile, it should be noted that the answers will depend on the specific properties of particular systems.

B. *Neglect of Oligopoly*

While neoclassical systems are almost invariably cast in a competitive environment, (more precisely, prices are given for producers and consumers), the existence of a solution for the case of general mono-

---

[3] Arrow and Hahn (1971) p. 29.

polistic competition, e.g. product differentiation, can be proved. No such solution can be proved to exist in the case of oligopoly, and in view of the particularistic nature of oligopolistic behaviour it seems most improbable that oligopoly can be incorporated successfully within a neoclassical system.

C. *Exclusion of the Future*

So far, no satisfactory method of incorporating uncertainty, risk, or expectations in the neoclassical system has been found.[4] This is one reason why the criticisms of that system made by Keynes (see chapter 8), cannot adequately be dealt with. Looking at the real world, it is probably significant that decentralised economic systems appear to have been on the whole less successful at maintaining a high rate of investment than centralised systems. The former are perhaps more vulnerable to uncertainty in their decision-making concerning the future.

D. *Institutional Biasses*

Having been developed by Walras as a model of the working of a market economy, neoclassical systems have been attacked as being implicitly biassed in favour of "the capitalist system",[5] or crudely, as being attempts at an intellectual justification of capitalism. Such criticisms appear to have three main strands. First, it is alleged that the analysis is not of general applicability because it is confined to one particular form of economic organisation, viz. the private ownership of the means of production. This criticism is certainly misplaced. Lange and Lerner, and more recently, Sik, Kyn and others have shown that a neoclassical general equilibrium analysis is equally applicable to an economy where the means of production are socially-owned, but where decision-making is decentralised, i.e. "market socialism." Even in a more centralised planned economy, the neoclassical analysis may be appropriate for the formulation of decision-rules. But in a command economy, where

[4] See, however, the work of Radner (1968).
[5] Critics do not usually take the trouble to define precisely what they mean by this phrase.

decision-making is completely centralised, neoclassical analysis would be clearly inappropriate. Even in a command economy, however, interdependence is unavoidable and allocative efficiency is probably desirable, so that other forms of general equilibrium analysis would be helpful in the formulation of plans. See part III.

Secondly, it is sometimes claimed that the particular set of prices and quantities which emerge as a solution to a neoclassical system depends upon the initial distribution of factor services. The resulting income distribution may not be socially acceptable, and therefore the associated price/quantity solution should not be accepted either. This may well be true, but the analysis has no preference for one solution rather than another. As we have shown on p. 31 fn. 7 an almost infinite number of solutions can be generated *either* by altering the initial distribution of factor services, $\bar{y}_{jk}$ in equation set (5.2) *or* by inserting an additional income distribution expression in the same set.

Finally, it is suggested that the existence of a solution with simultaneous price and quantity equilibrium in all markets dwells with disproportionate emphasis on apparently harmonious aspects of reality. At the same time, it ignores such disharmonious aspects as perhaps an increasing tendency towards inequality of incomes, concentration of ownership of assets, monetary instability, low rates of growth, etc. etc. It is certainly true that the neoclassical analysis does not deal with questions of growth, absolute prices, nor changes in economic organisation. Nor does any other theory of value. It is a misunderstanding of the concept of equilibrium to suggest that it carries any normative connotation; it is a methodological device, nothing more.

E. *Non-operationalism*

In principle, a neoclassical system incorporates an unlimited number of goods and households. But few would suggest that it would be possible ever to obtain the data to estimate empirically the parameters of all of the functions and relations in a modern economy. The neoclassical analysis of general equilibrium is therefore confined to the realm of pure theory, an elegant structure indeed, but with little hope of direct implementation or testing.

The foregoing criticisms of the neoclassical analysis of general equilibrium should not blind us to the fact that we can construct general equilibrium systems on other assumptions which are free of these defects. These alternative systems, which we have labelled "classical", are less powerful in an explanatory sense but they are more robust. A detailed comparison of the main differences between the two kinds of system is given in chapter 12 and classical systems are discussed in chapters 13 to 16. However, we have still to look at the uses of the neoclassical analysis. In subsequent chapters in Part II we discuss the introduction of money into the system, the criticisms of Keynes, and applications of the analysis to welfare economics and to the theory of international trade. But first, a clearer understanding of the significance of a neoclassical system may be obtained with the help of a very crude numerical example.

An Example

In this example, there are only two commodities, two inputs, and two households. The number of firms is unspecified. In order to obtain a particular solution we must assign specific forms to the utility and production functions.

Let the utility function of the first household be written

$$U_1 = b_1 q_{11}^A q_{21}^B \tag{1}$$

and that of the second household

$$U_2 = b_2 q_{12}^A q_{22}^B \tag{2}$$

Neither household saves, so their respective budget constraints can be written:

$$z_1 = p_1 q_{11} + p_2 q_{21} \tag{3}$$

$$z_2 = p_1 q_{12} + p_2 q_{22} \tag{4}$$

Each household maximises its utility subject to its budget constraint. When the utility functions are of the type shown in (1) and (2) then demand functions of the type (5) to (8) below can be derived as follows:

For the first household maximise

$$U_1 = b_1 q_{11}^A q_{21}^B \qquad \text{subject to} \qquad z_1 = p_1 q_{11} + p_2 q_{21}$$

Form the expression

$$U = b_1 q_{11}^A q_{21}^B + \lambda(z_1 - p_1 q_{11} - p_2 q_{21})$$

$$\therefore \quad \frac{\partial U}{\partial q_{11}} = A b_1 q_{11}^{A-1} q_{21}^B - \lambda p_1 = 0$$

and

$$\frac{\partial U}{\partial q_{21}} = B b_1 q_{11}^A q_{21}^{B-1} - \lambda p_2 = 0$$

and

$$\frac{\partial U}{\partial \lambda} = z_1 - p_1 q_{11} - p_2 q_{21} = 0$$

Eliminating λ from the first two of these first-order conditions, we have

$$\frac{1}{p_1} \cdot A b_1 q_{11}^{A-1} q_{21}^B = \frac{1}{p_2} \cdot B b_1 q_{11}^A q_{21}^{B-1}$$

$$\therefore \quad \frac{p_2}{p_1} \cdot \frac{A}{B} \cdot q_{11}^{-1} q_{21} = 1$$

From the third equation, we have

$$q_{21} = \frac{z_1 - p_1 q_{11}}{p_2}$$

and substituting for q_{21}, we then have

$$\frac{p_2}{p_1} \cdot \frac{A}{B} \cdot q_{11}^{-1} \cdot \frac{(z_1 - p_1 q_{11})}{p_2} = 1$$

$$\therefore \quad \frac{1}{p_1} \cdot \frac{A}{B} \cdot \left(\frac{z_1}{q_{11}} - p_1 \right) = 1$$

Hence,

$$q_{11} = \frac{A}{A+B} \cdot \frac{z_1}{p_1}$$

The other three demand equations may be obtained similarly.

Because of the specific form of the utility function, the demand functions for each goods have as arguments only the *own* price of the goods. Generally, they are functions of *all* goods prices: See equations on p. 34, set (5.1)

Demand Equations for Consumer Goods

$$q_{11} = \frac{A}{A+B} \frac{z_1}{p_1} \tag{5}$$

$$q_{21} = \frac{B}{A+B} \frac{z_1}{p_2} \tag{6}$$

$$q_{12} = \frac{A}{A+B} \frac{z_2}{p_1} \tag{7}$$

$$q_{22} = \frac{B}{A+B} \frac{z_2}{p_2} \tag{8}$$

Equilibrium Conditions for Consumers

The two inputs are available in fixed supply. For simplicity, we suppose that the entire supply of the first input is owned by the first household and the second by the second household.

$$z_1 = r_1 y_1 \tag{9}$$

$$z_2 = r_2 y_2 \tag{10}$$

Relationships in Production

The two goods are produced, respectively, with production functions of the following form:

$$x_1 = a_1 y_{11}^{\alpha_1} y_{21}^{\beta_1} \qquad (\alpha_1 + \beta_1 = 1) \tag{11}$$

and

$$x_2 = a_2 y_{12}^{\alpha_2} y_{22}^{\beta_2} \qquad (\alpha_2 + \beta_2 = 1) \tag{12}$$

Each firm maximises its profits. From the familiar first order conditions for a profit maximum when the production functions are (11) and (12), then the demand functions for inputs may be obtained as follows: The profit function for a firm making commodity 1 with the production function of the form (11) is

$$\pi = p_1 a_1 y_{11}^{\alpha_1} y_{21}^{1-\alpha_1} - r_1 y_{11} - r_2 y_{21} - b$$

$$\therefore \quad \frac{\partial \pi}{\partial y_{11}} = \alpha_1 p_1 a_1 y_{11}^{\alpha_1 - 1} y_{21}^{1-\alpha_1} - r_1 = 0$$

and

$$\frac{\partial \pi}{\partial y_{21}} = (1 - \alpha_1) p_1 a_1 y_{11}^{\alpha_1} y_{21}^{-\alpha_1} - r_2 = 0$$

Recalling (11), these first-order conditions become:

$$\alpha_1 p_1 \frac{x_1}{y_{11}} - r_1 = 0$$

and

$$(1 - \alpha_1) p_1 \frac{x_1}{y_{21}} - r_2 = 0$$

Rearranging terms, the demand functions for the two inputs in the production of commodity 1 are respectively:

$$y_{11} = p_1 \frac{\alpha_1}{r_1} x_1$$

and

$$y_{21} = p_1 \frac{\beta_1}{r_2} x_1$$

The other two input demand functions may be obtained similarly.

Demand Equations for Inputs of Factor Services

$$y_{11} = p_1 \frac{\alpha_1}{r_1} x_1 \qquad (13)$$

$$y_{21} = p_1 \frac{\beta_1}{r_2} x_1 \qquad (14)$$

$$y_{12} = p_2 \frac{\alpha_2}{r_1} x_2 \tag{15}$$

$$y_{22} = p_2 \frac{\beta_2}{r_2} x_2 \tag{16}$$

Production Equilibrium Conditions

Both production functions are homogeneous of degree one. Adding together equations (9) and (10) shows that total profits must be zero. This implies that the number of firms and their size remains undetermined. It also indicates that the long-run zero profit conditions, equations (5.4) on page 34 would be superfluous in this example, since the conditions are already implicit in the other equations. We therefore replace these with the two production functions which we incorporate directly in our system.

Commodity Market Clearing Equations

The prices of the two goods adjust in order that the total demand should just be equal to output

$$q_{11} + q_{12} = x_1 \tag{17}$$

$$q_{21} + q_{22} = x_2 \tag{18}$$

Factor Market Clearing Equations

The prices of the two inputs adjust so that the total supply of each input is fully absorbed in production.

$$y_{11} + y_{12} = y_1 \tag{19}$$

$$y_{21} + y_{22} = y_2 \tag{20}$$

A Numerical Solution

There are sixteen variables whose values are to be determined:

The quantities of the two goods produced	x_1, x_2
The prices of the goods	p_1, p_2

The quantities of each good consumed by
each household $q_{11}, q_{12}, q_{21}, q_{22}$

The quantities of the inputs absorbed in the
production of each good $y_{11}, y_{12}, y_{21}, y_{22}$

The prices of the inputs r_1, r_2

The income of each household z_1, z_2

We have sixteen equations, viz. (5) to (20) inclusive, which might be
expected, with given values for the parameters, to determine a solution.
However, it can easily be shown that the sixteen equations are not
independent: for example, equation (18) can be derived from the
remaining fifteen equations. Thus we have only fifteen independent
equations and sixteen variables. We can eliminate one variable by
putting the price of the first input, r_1, equal to 1.

There are three sets of parameters:

Technology: the coefficients a_j, α_j, and β_j

Preferences: the coefficients A and B

Resources: the input supply totals y_j

Suppose that we are given the following values for these parameters:

$a_1 = a_2 = 1.1$; $\alpha_1 = 0.24$; $\alpha_2 = 0.225$; $\beta_1 = 0.76$; $\beta_2 = 0.775$;
$A = 0.5$; $B = 0.25$; $y_1 = 200$; $y_2 = 400$:

Then, putting $r_1 = 1$, the following values can be found to satisfy the
equations of the system.

$x_1 = 248.11$ $x_2 = 125.69$

$p_1 = 2.29$ $p_2 = 2.26$

$q_{11} = 58.2$ $q_{21} = 29.5$ $q_{12} = 189.9$ $q_{22} = 96.16$

$y_{11} = 136.0$ $y_{12} = 64.0$ $y_{21} = 264.8$ $y_{22} = 135.2$

$r_2 = 1.63$

$z_1 = 200.0$ $z_2 = 652.0$

With this example it is easy to check the zero homogeneity property of
prices in the neoclassical system. By simply multiplying each of the
goods and input prices by a common factor, the equations will still be
seen to hold and the solution for the quantities of inputs and outputs
will remain unchanged.

6 The Existence, Uniqueness and Stability of Equilibrium

This chapter is different in style from those which have gone before, and from those which follow. Its function is mainly definitional: to clarify certain concepts which are in use throughout the book, and indeed are commonplace—but often misunderstood—in economic analysis generally. The chapter has a second function: to summarise in very simple terms the economic significance of the work which has been done under this chapter heading in the last two decades.[1]

Let us begin with a definition of equilibrium. The concept has been borrowed from classical mechanics where it is stated:

> A configuration is one of equilibrium if the system can remain indefinitely in this configuration under the forces acting upon it.

This definition[2] brings out two significant features of equilibrium from the point of view of economic analysis. First, the idea of a balance of forces, and secondly, the implication that equilibrium is essentially a dynamic concept, even when it appears in a static analysis.

Economic models or systems may have specific solutions in which the variables are at rest, i.e. have no tendency to change their value, but

---

[1] Those who wish to acquaint themselves with this work, and who feel equipped to follow the set theoretic approach, might begin with Quirk and Saposnick (1968) before going on to read Arrow and Hahn (1971).

[2] Rutherford (1957), p. 119; cf. Pareto's definition of economic equilibrium, quoted by Kuenne (1967) p. 18: "(equilibrium is) a specific solution to an economic model describing a state of rest and resulting from the opposition between identifiable desires of men and obstacles to their fulfilment".

unless this solution is the outcome of an opposition of identifiable forces it cannot be described as an equilibrium. Many models based on the prediction of routine behaviour, for example this period's price equals last period's price plus 10% are not equilibrium models according to this definition.

The concept of equilibrium may be regarded as dynamic in the sense that some underlying notion of the out-of-equilibrium behaviour of the system is implied. Thus in the simplest case, a single market is said to be in equilibrium if the quantity supplied equals the quantity demanded. This apparently static definition is based on the supposition that if quantities supplied and demanded are *not* equal, price will tend to change in a predictable way. To take an example from macroeconomic theory: where equilibrium is defined in terms of expectations fulfilled, some disequilibrium behaviour is implied concerning the revision of unsatisfied expectations.

Existence of Equilibrium in a Single Market

An equilibrium in a single market can be said to exist if there are one or more non-negative prices at which quantities supplied and demanded are equal and nonnegative.

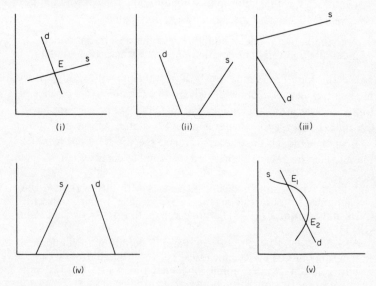

Fig. 6.1

In Fig. 6.1(i) a single equilibrium in the sense defined occurs at E. In case (ii), the supply exceeds the demand at a zero price, and in this case we describe the good in question as a *free good*. Fresh air and agricultural crops, once produced, may sometimes be free goods. For example, once a fruit crop has been grown, a certain quantity may be available costlessly, but additional supplies may depend upon costs of storage and refrigeration. While case (ii) does not strictly correspond to our definition of equilibrium, we can regard this case as being consistent with equilibrium if the excess supply at a zero price can be disposed of without cost. In case (iii) we have a situation in which there is no quantity at which the price suppliers are willing to accept does not exceed the price potential consumers are willing to pay. Here no equilibrium solution is possible, and the good is not produced. Gold bathtubs might be an example of a *non-produced* good. In a general equilibrium analysis, as opposed to the partial equilibrium analysis represented by the diagrams, one cannot determine in advance which goods are free goods, which are non-produced, and which are "normal" goods, because this depends partly on the set of relative prices which are simultaneously determined in the equilibrium solution.

There is no equilibrium either in case (iv). It is difficult to think of any actual situation to which this case might correspond, and therefore we may ignore it. Finally, in Fig. 6.1(v), there are two points of equilibrium, E_1 and E_2, where the backward-bending supply curve twice cuts the demand curve.

Existence of Equilibrium in a System of Markets

There are two views about the desirability of proving the existence of solutions to general equilibrium systems. The first view is expressed by Dorfman, Samuelson and Solow (1958) when they write:

> . . . a system of equations whose assumptions do not guarantee the existence of a solution may fail to be a useful idealisation of reality.[3]

[3] As Kuenne (1967) points out (p. 20), the reference to reality may be misleading, since what is at issue is a property of the model, not of reality: ". . . the assumptions concerning continuity of function and correspondence which must be made to guarantee the existence of equilibrium in such static model approximations to reality may be more accurately described as a retreat from reality, not a guarantee that it has been approached."

They criticise the custom of counting equations and variables, pointing out quite rightly that an equality between the numbers of equations and variables is neither necessary nor sufficient for the existence of a solution.

Against this it may be argued that a model can have value even if it should be impossible to prove the existence of a solution to it. It may be necessary to sacrifice operationalism in order to represent the complexities of interdependence. And while counting equations and variables can prove nothing positively it does reveal whether the system is consistent with the existence of equilibrium.

Undoubtedly, the second view is intellectually less satisfying, but it is broadly the one which we take in this book. Our purpose is purely expository, and in view of the much greater "intellectual coarseness", to borrow a phrase of Hahn's, displayed by other textbooks in dividing economic analysis into separate compartments labelled macro-economics and microeconomics, we feel no need to make apologies. In presenting different systems of general equilibrium we shall describe sufficient conditions for existence, where these have been proved.

In the case of neoclassical general equilibrium, existence proofs have been given by Arrow and Debreu (1954), Nikaido (1956), Arrow and Hahn (1971) and others. Each proof has started from different assumptions, but the flavour of those theorems can be indicated by a description of the Arrow–Debreu proof. The first thing which needs to be said about the Arrow–Debreu proof is that it was concerned only with existence, and not with uniqueness or stability properties.

Among the characteristics of the Arrow–Debreu model economy are the following:

(a) production is characterised by nonincreasing returns to scale;
(b) all markets are perfect;
(c) the supply of factor services may not be perfectly inelastic;
(d) profits need not be zero, but may be negative;
(e) firms may produce more than one product;
(f) individual consumer demands depend not only on income but also on wealth.

Their choice of assumptions is dictated by the desire to rule out all circumstances in which an equilibrium might fail to be realised. Thus if assumption (a) were violated by permitting increasing returns to scale generally, then it might prove impossible to realise in some sectors the production equilibrium condition, total revenue = total cost. Yet none of the assumptions listed are any more restrictive than those we have discussed so far. Indeed, Arrow and Hahn (1971) have recently proved the existence of a general equilibrium for an economy with limited increasing returns and monopolistic competition.

There is one assumption which Arrow and Debreu are forced to make, however, which may be more difficult to accept. Every consumer is assumed initially to possess stocks of *every* commodity and factor service large enough to permit every consumer to supply some of every good and every factor service to the market under any permissible set of prices. This bizarre assumption is needed in the Arrow-Debreu model to guarantee continuity in all circumstances of the aggregate supply and demand functions. Without it, a set of prices might emerge which would leave some households with zero incomes and thus permit the possibility of a discontinuity in the demand function for one or more commodities. While such a stringent assumption has been modified in subsequent proofs, it remains generally true that the continuity requirement is the reason for the most restrictive assumptions in proofs of existence. Thus, existence proofs which use calculus methods depend upon the "well-behaved" property in continuous production functions.

Stability of Equilibrium

It is one question whether an equilibrium exists. It is quite another whether the system will attain that equilibrium, even if it can be shown to exist. This is the question of stability. Walras having solved, as he thought, the question of the existence of a solution to a general equilibrium system by equation-counting then addressed himself to the question of stability. Supposing that the system was initially out of equilibrium, Walras envisaged that an equilibrium would eventually be attained by an iterative process. Suppose that an external agency moves through each market in turn, adjusting each price to its equilibrium value. When the process is complete the last market will be in equilibrium, and, because of interdependence among markets, all the others will be out of equilibrium; but, Walras conjectured, not by as much as before. This was because he assumed that supply and demand responded more to "own-price" changes than to "other-price" changes. If the process were repeated, the system would eventually reach equilibrium. In the real world, this equilibrium would be realised in an unplanned way by trial and error, or groping (tâtonnement) by the market mechanism. While, in theory, this process of eventual adjust-

ment may take place timelessly, in practice it would be difficult to maintain that it would not use up real time.

At the beginning of this chapter, it was stated that equilibrium was a dynamic concept even when it appears in a static analysis. What is meant by "static" and "dynamic"? A dynamic model or system may be defined as one into which time enters in an essential and meaningful way, and the solution to which is a path through time. A static system may be regarded as the special case of a corresponding dynamic system, in which the values of all the variables repeat themselves in every period of time. The connection between the analysis of stability and dynamic systems may be summarised in the following way. While one may justifiably speak of the *existence* of an equilibrium for a *static* system, one should properly speak of the *stability* of an equilibrium only for a corresponding *dynamic* system. This point may be illustrated with the case of a single market.

Stability Analysis of a Single Market

Consider the following static system:

A linear market demand function,

$$q(p) = a_1 p + b_1 \tag{6.1}$$

A linear market supply function,

$$x(p) = a_2 p + b_2 \tag{6.2}$$

The market equilibrium condition,

$$q(p) = x(p) \tag{6.3}$$

Solving this system, the expressions for the equilibrium price, $\bar{p}$, and the equilibrium quantity, $\bar{q}$, turn out to be:

$$\bar{p} = \frac{b_1 - b_2}{a_2 - a_1} \tag{6.4}$$

$$\bar{q} = \frac{a_2 b_1 - a_1 b_2}{a_2 - a_1} \tag{6.5}$$

But this equation system tells us nothing of the behaviour of the market when it is out of equilibrium, i.e. when some price prevails at which demand and supply are not equal. Since the study of the stability of an equilibrium is nothing but a study of the consequences of a displacement from it, we cannot properly discuss stability without introducing an explicit mechanism describing the out-of equilibrium behaviour of the system. Let this be represented by the following differential equation

$$\frac{dp}{dt} = \kappa[q(p) - x(p)] \qquad \kappa > 0 \tag{6.6}$$

Equation (6.6) states that the rate of increase of price is directly proportional to the size of excess demand, κ being the coefficient of proportionality. This equation, then, embodies an hypothesis about the response of price to an initial imbalance between the quantities supplied and demanded. The particular hypothesis expressed by (6.6) is known as Walras' Excess Demand Hypothesis.

Substituting the "disequilibrium" equation (6.6) for the equilibrium condition (6.3), consider the dynamic system of equations formed by (6.1), (6.2), and (6.6). Substituting (6.1) and (6.2) into (6.6), we have

$$\frac{dp}{dt} + \kappa(a_2 - a_1)p = \kappa(b_1 - b_2) \tag{6.7}$$

(6.7) is a first order linear differential equation, having the general solution[4]

---

[4] To obtain (6.8) from (6.7) proceed as follows:
Put $z = \kappa(a_1 - a_2)$, Divide (6.7) by z and re-arrange terms.
Then

$$\frac{1}{z}\frac{dp}{dt} - p = \frac{b_1 - b_2}{a_1 - a_2}$$

But

$$\bar{p} = -\frac{(b_1 - b_2)}{a_1 - a_2}$$

$$\therefore \quad \frac{dp}{dt} = z(p - \bar{p})$$

Now write $\hat{p} = (p - \bar{p})$ and note that $d\hat{p}/dt = dp/dt$

$$\therefore \quad \frac{d\hat{p}}{dt} = z\hat{p}$$

$$p_t = \frac{b_1 - b_2}{a_2 - a_1} + ce^{-\kappa(a_2 - a_1)t} \tag{6.8}$$

where c is a constant of integration. Putting $t = 0$, we get

$$p_0 = \frac{b_1 - b_2}{a_2 - a_1} + c \tag{6.9}$$

but from (6.4) we know that

$$\bar{p} = \frac{b_1 - b_2}{a_2 - a_1},$$

so that

$$c = p_0 - \bar{p} \tag{6.10}$$

Therefore equation (6.8) can be rewritten as

$$p_t = \bar{p} - (\bar{p} - p_0)e^{-\kappa(a_2 - a_1)t} \tag{6.11}$$

From (6.11) it can be seen that *if*

$$(a_2 - a_1) > 0 \tag{6.12}$$

$\therefore \quad \dfrac{1}{\hat{p}} \dfrac{d\hat{p}}{dt} = z$

$\therefore \quad \dfrac{d(\log \hat{p})}{dt} = z$

$\therefore \quad \int (\log \hat{p})dt = \int z \, dt$

$\therefore \quad \log \hat{p} = k + zt$

$\therefore \quad \hat{p} = e^{(k + zt)} = ce^{zt}$

But

$\hat{p} = p - \bar{p}$

$\therefore \quad (p - \bar{p}) = ce^{k(a_1 - a_2)t}$

$\therefore \quad p_t = \bar{p} + ce^{k(a_1 - a_2)t}$

$\therefore \quad p_t = \dfrac{b_1 - b_2}{a_2 - a_1} + ce^{-\kappa(a_2 - a_1)t}$

then, as $t \to \infty$

$$p_t = \bar{p} \tag{6.13}$$

Thus we have shown that *if* (a) the out-of-equilibrium behaviour of the market is actually described by equation (6.6), *and if* (b), equation (6.12) is satisfied, then the market will eventually return to equilibrium following some displacement, or from some initial disequilibrium. But notice that this will only be true provided both conditions (a) and (b) are satisfied.

It is customary to refer to (b) as the "stability condition" of the system. Since equation (6.12) is an expression in the parameters of the static system, (6.1), (6.2), (6.3), this has led many people including Walras, Marshall, and Hicks, to make the mistake of supposing that the stability or otherwise of the market equilibrium can be inferred from the static system of equations alone. This is the same as saying that the stability of equilibrium can be inferred from the slopes of the demand and supply curves in the traditional market diagram.

But this supposition overlooks the fact that the particular form of the stability conditions expressed in (6.12) is derived from the particular form assigned to the equation (6.6) describing the out-of-equilibrium behaviour of the system. Had we chosen a different hypothesis for out-of-equilibrium behaviour, then (6.12) would have been different. Consider, for example, the dynamic system of market behaviour represented by the equations:

$$q_t(p) = a_1 p_t + b_1 \tag{6.14}$$

$$x_t(p) = a_2 p_{t-1} + b_2 \tag{6.15}$$

$$q_t(p) = x_t(p) \tag{6.16}$$

This is the well-known "cobweb" model, with a one-period lag in the supply function. Given some initial price, the following period's supply is determined by (6.15). Equation (6.16) requires that the market be cleared, and therefore price will adjust itself to bring demand into equality with supply. This price will then determine the supply of the next period. Solving this dynamic system in the usual way, it turns out that it will converge to the static equilibrium, *if*

$$\frac{a_2}{a_1} > 1 \tag{6.17}$$

This stability condition is different from (6.12), yet *both* dynamic systems can be regarded as corresponding to the static system (6.1), (6.2), (6.3). We can see that the static system is a special case of (6.1), (6.2), (6.6), by putting the value $dp/dt = 0$ in (6.6), which gives $q(p) = x(p)$ in that equation, which makes it the same as (6.3). Likewise, by putting the special value $p_{t-1} = p_t$ in equation (6.15) then the dynamic system (6.14), (6.15), (6.16) degenerates to the same static system.

Thus we can see that there is more than one dynamic system which has (6.1), (6.2), (6.3), as its corresponding static system. Therefore we cannot infer anything about the stability of the equilibrium of a static system until a corresponding dynamic system, which is implied by the question of disequilibrium behaviour, i.e. by the question of stability, has been explicitly specified.

Stability in a System of Markets

We have seen, in the case of only a single market that it is necessary to introduce a dynamic system to analyse the question of stability of market equilibrium. Strictly speaking, a fully satisfactory dynamic analysis has three essential components: (i) a specification of the initial conditions, (ii) a specification of the out-of-equilibrium behaviour or error-adjustment mechanism, (iii) a solution which gives the time paths of the appropriate variables. It is hardly necessary to emphasise further the difficulties which lie in the way of any attempts at rigorous proofs of stability properties of systems of general equilibrium of the neo-classical type. Certainly, little can be said about the stability (or the uniqueness) properties of systems based on relatively non restrictive assumptions such as those used by Arrow and Debreu to prove theorems about the existence of equilibrium.

But theorems about the stability of general systems have been proved for a limited number of special cases of quite restricted generality.[5] They fall into two classes. First, assuming some specific form of out-of-equilibrium behaviour, (usually the Walrasian excess demand hypothesis), the behaviour of the resulting dynamic system is

---

[5] Strictly speaking, these theorems, mainly by Arrow and Hurwicz (1958), Metzler (1945), Morishima (1960), and others have been proved about the stability of multiple exchange systems which may be regarded as reduced forms of neoclassical general equilibrium systems. See chapter seven.

investigated. Theorems are then proved about the conditions under which an equilibrium in whose neighborhood the system is defined is a stable one. The second class of stability theorems concerns such questions as what kind of general equilibrium systems are likely to have equilibria which satisfy these conditions. Investigating such questions Arrow and Hurwicz found that in none of their selected cases was a neoclassical system shown to be unstable. However, counter examples have been constructed leading Kuenne (1967) p. 508, to observe

> ... a potential route out of such system instability is to overthrow the assumption that market equilibrium is attained in a recontracting tâtonnement process, and to substitute for it an equilibrating process which permits non-equilibrium transactions to occur. Non-tâtonnement equilibrium may prove to be the answer.

Certainly, the tâtonnement process is an unsatisfactory device, evading as it does the adjustment issue. It may be significant that the literature on non-equilibrium behaviour has recently been expanding. See chapter 8 below.

Two results of the investigations into stability properties of neo-classical systems may be worth mentioning. Under the usual dis-equilibrium behaviour assumptions, and the usual properties of a neoclassical general equilibrium system, an equilibrium of the corresponding dynamic system is locally stable if all commodities are strict gross substitutes.[6] Secondly, it can be shown that if a system satisfies the weak axiom of revealed preference in the aggregate,[7] then it is globally stable (i.e. it will return to the initial equilibrium following a disturbance of any magnitude).

[6] If the excess demand for commodity i is written E_i then all goods are gross substitutes if

$$\frac{\partial E_i}{\partial p_j} < 0 \qquad \text{for all} \qquad i = j$$

and

$$\frac{\partial E_i}{\partial p_j} > 0 \qquad \text{for all} \qquad i \neq j$$

[7] The weak axiom of revealed preference can be stated as follows: if p_i^0 and q_i^0 are prices and quantities satisfying demand functions, and p_i^1 and q_i^1 are another such set, then $\Sigma p_i^0 q_i^0 \geqslant \Sigma p_i^0 q_i^1$ must imply that $\Sigma p_i^1 q_i^1 < \Sigma p_i^1 q_i^0$. Applied to the individual consumer's demand function this axiom implies nothing more than behaviour consistent with an un-

In general, we may conclude that in a neoclassical general equilibrium system with the familiar disequilibrium behaviour assumption, if second order equilibrium conditions are fulfilled by all the relevant functions, the equilibrium attained will *probably* be stable.

Uniqueness of Equilibrium

Uniqueness is a property of an equilibrium solution which is of less interest than either existence or stability. It is true that *local* uniqueness may be a desirable property if one is carrying out a comparative static analysis. Otherwise it is not all evident that it is a particularly desirable property. However it can be proved that if an equilibrium exists for a system characterised *either* by gross substitutability *or* by the weak axiom holding for aggregate excess demands, then that equilibrium is unique. In the case of a unique equilibrium with global stability, one may speak of stability of the *system*. Otherwise, one should speak of the (local) stability of a particular *equilibrium*. Uniqueness proofs do have the further disadvantage that they require restrictions which are not intuitively acceptable. The "well-behaved" property of the production function, for example, excludes a wide range of plausible production behaviour.

---

changing set of preferences. But applied "in the aggregate", i.e. to market demand functions, it is a very strong assumption indeed. It implies that the economy as a whole has a single set of "preferences", which are unchanged as prices change. Normally, one would expect changes in price to change the distribution of income, and hence changing "preferences" would be revealed.

7 Money and the Neoclassical System

The functions of money in an economic system have been divided traditionally into three: (i) money as a standard of value, (or unit of account), (ii) money as a store of value, and (iii) money as a medium of exchange. In this chapter, we shall examine the ways in which neo-classical theorists have attempted to incorporate a theory of money, (i.e. a theory of absolute prices), into their theory of value, (i.e. a theory of relative prices as determined in a general equilibrium system).

If we confine money to its role as a unit of account, there are no difficulties at all. Indeed, we have been treating money exactly in this way in our discussion so far. We have expressed prices in money terms, yet we have not allowed money to exist as a commodity. We have implicitly assumed hitherto that no one holds money nor desires to do so. Goods therefore exchange for goods, and money has no function as a store of value nor as a medium of exchange. Economic systems based upon such assumptions are sometimes called "real" systems to distinguish them from monetary systems.

Let us see how we can use money as an accounting device before introducing it as a commodity.

Money as a Unit of Account

A relative price is an exchange ratio between two goods. If 2 tons of wheat exchange for 1 machine, the price of wheat in terms of machines is $\frac{1}{2}$. If we use one good, v as a benchmark or *numéraire*, and if there are n goods in the economic system, then there are $(n-1)$ independent exchange ratios, each of the form

$$p_i/p_v$$

Any good can serve as *numéraire*, and the change of *numéraire* leaves the exchange ratios between other goods unaffected. Relative prices can be expressed in money terms by setting the price of the numéraire equal to a specified number of monetary units. Thus if v is the numéraire and p_v is set equal to £b, then the price of any other good, $\hat{p}_i$, can be expressed in money terms as

$$\hat{p}_i = b \cdot p_i/p_v \tag{7.1}$$

The relative price of a good in terms of money is its absolute price.

It will be recalled that in the discussion of our neoclassical system in chapter five, it was argued that there were only $(N - 1)$ independent equations in the system. From the budgetary balance of each household implied in (5.2) together with the zero profit condition for each firm (5.4), we can deduce that the market value of aggregate supply in such systems must be equal to the market value of aggregate demand. The budget equation for each household, k, can be written formally as

$$\sum_{i=1}^{n} q_{ik} p_i \equiv \sum_{j=1}^{m} r_j y_{jk} \tag{7.2}$$

Summing over all households gives the aggregate budget restriction

$$\sum_{k=1}^{s} \sum_{i=1}^{n} q_{ik} p_i \equiv \sum_{k=1}^{s} \sum_{j=1}^{m} r_j y_{jk} \tag{7.3}$$

The left-hand term in (7.3) represents the total value of purchases by all households, and the right-hand term is the total value of all factor incomes. The expression may be interpreted to mean that in a general equilibrium system where money appears only as a unit of account, the market value of aggregate supply is *identically* equal to the market value of aggregate demand. This is sometimes known as *Walras' Law*. The significance of the identity[1] is that the expression holds true for *all values* of the prices, not just the equilibrium values. Within the assumptions of this system, there is *no possibility* of a discrepancy arising between the values of aggregate supply and aggregate demand.

---

[1] We may give an algebraic illustration of the distinction between an identity and an equality. The identity $(a + b)^2 \equiv a^2 + 2ab + b^2$ is true for all values of a and b, whereas the equality $a - 2b = 3$ is true only for certain values of a and b.

Money as a Store of Value

The function of money as a store of value has some intertemporal implications. We postpone these for the moment and consider first the transactions motive for holding money as a commodity. It will simplify our discussion of the introduction of commodity money into a neoclassical system of general equilibrium if we modify that system so that supplies of goods are taken as given, and concentrate on the exchange aspects. The problems which arise fall mainly in the area of exchange rather than production.

The Pure Exchange System

Assume that there are stocks of n produced goods or factor services held by consumers in the economy. Then we can write n market demand equations, each of the form

$$q_i = q_i(p_i, p_2, \ldots, p_n) \tag{7.4}$$

and n market supply equations, each of the form

$$x_i = x_i(p_1, p_2, \ldots, p_n) \tag{7.5}$$

Defining the excess demand, E_i, for any good i as the difference between the quantity demanded and the quantity supplied at *any* set of prices

$$E_i = q_i(p_1, p_2, \ldots, p_n) - x_i(p_1, p_2, \ldots, p_n) \tag{7.6}$$

it is clear that the excess demand for any good i, must be a function of the set of prices, and that the equilibrium condition for market i must be that excess demand be zero, so that for a general equilibrium

$$E_i = 0 \qquad (i = 1, \ldots, n) \tag{7.7}$$

Money as a Commodity

Let us now introduce money as a commodity (currency) into our pure exchange system, and denote it as good $(n + 1)$. By definition, $p_{n+1} = 1$, and therefore it can be omitted in writing the set of prices $(p_1, p_2, \ldots, p_n)$. Each consumer, in addition to initial stocks of the n goods, now has an initial stock of money, $q_{n+1,k}^0$. The k'th consumer's

excess demand for money can be defined as the stock of money he
desires to hold less his initial stock:

$$E_{n+1,k} = q_{n+1,k} - q^0_{n+1,k} \tag{7.8}$$

If the individual consumer tries to add to his initial stock of money, his
excess demand for money is said to be positive and the value of goods
he sells is greater than the value he buys. Thus the consumer cannot
alter his excess demand for money without altering his excess demand
for at least one other good.

But what determines the consumer's excess demand for money?
Given some arbitrary initial supply of money (as we have assumed), this
amounts to asking what determines the consumers demand for money?
The consumer's demand for the other n goods in the system is determined by utility maximisation but a basic principle of neoclassical
thinking is that money should not enter the consumer's utility
function. Let us assume instead that the consumer's need for money for
transactions purposes will be satisfied by his holding a quantity of
money which is a fixed proportion of the money value of his initial
stock of goods, i.e.

$$q_{n+1,k} = \alpha_k \sum_{i=1}^{n} p_i q^0_{ik} \tag{7.9}$$

where α_k is some arbitrary constant. Substituting this expression for
$q_{n+1,k}$ in (7.8), we have the individual consumer's excess demand for
money

$$E_{n+1,k} = \alpha_k \sum_{i=1}^{n} p_i q^0_{ik} - q^0_{n+1,k} \tag{7.10}$$

Summing (7.10) for all consumers gives the following expression for the
aggregate excess demand for money

$$E_{n+1} = \alpha_k \sum_{k=1}^{s} \sum_{i=1}^{n} p_i q^0_{ik} - \sum_{k=1}^{s} q^0_{n+1,k} \tag{7.11}$$

Assuming that the initial distribution of stocks of goods and money
(q^0_{ik} and $q^0_{n+1,k}$) is fixed and that $\alpha_k = \alpha$ for all k,[2] then (7.11) can be
written

$$E_{n+1} = E_{n+1}(p_1, p_2, \ldots, p_n) \tag{7.12}$$

[2] This assumption is made for simplicity and involves no significant
loss of generality.

i.e. the aggregate excess demand for money is a function of the set of the money prices of the n goods in the system.

Let us now consider some of the properties of this system in which money appears as a commodity and compare them with the "real" neoclassical system set out in chapter 5, in which money appeared only as a unit of account. The definition of a general equilibrium in a pure exchange system is that the excess demand for each good and money (where it appears) should equal zero simultaneously

$$E_i(p_1, p_2, \ldots, p_n) = 0 \qquad (i = 1, 2, \ldots, n+1) \tag{7.13}$$

In chapter 5, it was shown that the values of quantities produced and consumed in a neoclassical system were determined by relative money prices. In a corresponding pure exchange system this can be translated by saying that excess demands for goods are homogeneous of degree zero in their prices. However, this is not true of the system once money has been introduced as a commodity. As one can see by multiplying all prices in (7.11) by some factor $t > 0$, an equiproportionate increase of all goods prices will increase the excess demand for money.[3] If the system was initially in equilibrium such an increase will lead consumers to want to exchange goods for money in order to bring their money stocks into line with the money value of their initial stocks of goods. In the absence of a negative excess demand for goods, the system will be thrown out of equilibrium. However, the "new" system, with the addition of money as a commodity, *is* homogeneous of degree zero in goods prices and initial money stocks.

The second important characteristic of the augmented system is that a proportionate change in the money stock of each consumer will result in an equiproportionate change in the money price of each good, but will leave the "real sector", i.e. quantities exchanged and relative prices, unaffected. This result is at first glance a congenial one: relative prices of goods in equilibrium remain determined by consumer's utility maximisation and the real values of their initial endowments. Money prices of goods (i.e. the absolute price level) are determined by the stock of money. Closer examination reveals a number of shortcomings. First, the apparent decomposability of the augmented system into a

[3] Notice that this result arises simply because we are treating money differently from all other commodities: if we were to increase the price of money equiproportionately with the price of goods, all excess demands, including that for money, would remain unchanged.

real part and a monetary part suggests that we have not got very far in our attempt to integrate value theory with monetary theory. Secondly, the monetary theory which is implied in our augmented system is trivial. Equilibrium in all goods markets implies a zero excess demand for money. This rules out the possibility, in equilibrium, of proceeds of sales of goods being used to increase cash holdings, or cash holdings being used to finance purchases. Why then do people hold money, how do they obtain it, and how do changes in the aggregate supply of money take place? On all these questions, our theory has nothing to say. Finally, our theory as embodied in the augmented system is open to the objection that a utility maximising consumer would have no reason to hold a stock of money from which he derives no utility rather than spend it on commodities from which he does. If money were introduced directly into the utility function, this might satisfy logic and end the dichotomy between real and monetary parts of the system. It was Patinkin who first took this step, but before looking at his system we should mention Say's Law.

Say's Law of Markets

Classical and neoclassical economists alike generally held the view that the aggregate excess demand for all goods taken together must be zero. In our notation

$$\sum_{i=1}^{n} p_i E_i = 0 \qquad (7.14)$$

This came to be known as Say's Law, although it was not always made clear whether it was to be interpreted as an identity or as an equilibrium condition.

In neoclassical systems where money appears only as a unit of account, and excess demand functions are homogeneous of degree zero in prices, it is evident that Say's Law holds true as an identity, and is logically equivalent to Walras' Law.

When money is introduced as a commodity, Say's Law implies that the excess demand for money is zero, otherwise the aggregate excess demand for goods must be non-zero. Interpreted as an equilibrium condition in this context, the augmented system is determined, and the absolute price level is determined by the quantity of money. However, if Say's Law should be interpreted as an identity, it means that the excess demand for money is identically equal to zero, and consumers will never desire to change their money stocks, regardless of the set of goods prices. Such implicit behaviour is not consistent with that described by (7.9), and the quantity of money cannot then serve to determine absolute price levels, which are indeterminate.

Patinkin's System

Does money confer any utility other than that derived from the goods on which it is spent? If, as most neoclassical economists tended to believe, the answer is "no", then there is no justification for going any further. If the answer is "yes", the question which immediately arises is "Why does money yield utility?" Let us postpone any answer to this question, and see what happens when we put money in the utility function, in the manner of Patinkin.

In chapter 1, we wrote the utility function of any consumer as

$$U_k = U_k(q_{1k}, q_{2k}, \ldots, q_{nk}) \tag{7.15}$$

Let us now replace this with

$$U_k = U_k\left(q_{1k}, q_{2k}, \ldots, q_{nk}, \frac{M_k}{p_0}\right) \tag{7.16}$$

where M_k is the stock of money held by the consumer, p^0 is some index of the general price level, e.g.

$$p^0 = \sum_{i=1}^{n} w_i p_i : \sum_{i=1}^{n} w_i = 1$$

and the term M_k/p^0 is known as the "real balance" of the consumer.

When the utility of each consumer is maximised subject to a budget constraint in which the cash holding enters, and the resulting demand and supply functions[4] are aggregated, the following system of equations emerges which we can call Patinkin's system.

[4] The aggregation of Patinkin's individual consumer demand functions for a specific commodity to form the aggregate market demand function for that commodity, as shown in equations (7.17), gives rise to a problem. Adding the individual demand functions yields a function of which the arguments are the set of relative prices and all the individual cash holdings, M_k. It is only legitimate to replace each of these variables with the aggregate $M = \Sigma_k M_k$, as in (7.17), if it can be assumed that demand for each good is unaffected by the distribution of cash between individuals.

Demand Equations

$$q_i = q_i(p_1/p^0, p_2/p^0, \ldots, p_n/p^0, M/p^0) \qquad (i = 1, \ldots, n) \quad (7.17)$$

$$q_m = q_m(p_1/p^0, p_2/p^0, \ldots, p_n/p^0, M/p^0) \qquad (7.18)$$

Supply Equations

$$x_i = x_i(p_1/p^0, p_2/p^0, \ldots, p_n/p^0, M/p^0) \qquad (i = 1, \ldots, n) \quad (7.19)$$

$$x_m = M/p^0 \qquad (7.20)$$

Equilibrium Conditions

$$q_i = x_i \qquad (i = 1, \ldots, n) \qquad (7.21)$$

$$q_m = x_m \qquad (7.22)$$

Price Index Equation

$$p^0 = \sum_{i=1}^{n} w_i p_i \qquad (7.23)$$

Thus, we have altogether $3n + 4$ equations to determine the $3n + 3$ unknown variables (nx's, nq's, np's and p^0, q_m, and x_m). Since real balances appear as an argument in the supply and demand functions for goods we cannot expect Say's Law to hold as an identity, but Walras' Law does hold which means that one of our equations is redundant, hence the system should be determinate.

An examination of the properties of this system shows that it has two in common with the augmented system represented in equation (7.13):

(1) Excess demands for goods and money are homogeneous of degree zero in the prices *and* the real balances.

(2) An increase in the quantity for money will increase all equilibrium money prices and the price level proportionately, while leaving all relative prices and goods quantities unaffected. Thus, despite money having been fully integrated into the neoclassical system, via the utility function of each consumer, in equilibrium it is still "neutral".

Yet in respect of stability, Patinkin's system represents an improvement on the augmented system. It will be recalled that an arbitrary rise in the general price level would throw the augmented system out of equilibrium with no indication as to how equilibrium might be regained. Compare what happens in Patinkin's system. Again assume that for a given value of aggregate M, all prices are quoted 10% above their equilibrium level. Relative prices remain unchanged, but real balances fall. This causes negative excess demand to arise in all goods markets. Assuming the response to this disequilibrium is represented by Walras' excess demand hypothesis, prices will begin to fall, and will continue to fall until the excess supplies have been eliminated and the original equilibrium restored.

It is instructive to see how, in Patinkin's system, the real balances play a role in the restoration of equilibrium when an initial equilibrium is disturbed by an increase of the money supply, M. Again, relative prices remain unchanged, but real balances have increased, thus excess demands arise in all goods markets. Applying Walras' hypothesis for disequilibrium behaviour, prices will tend to rise everywhere. The price increases will cause real balances to fall, and this process will continue for as long as real balances are larger than in the initial equilibrium. Prices will continue to rise until they have risen in proportion to the quantity of money, and so brought real balances down to their initial value.

Money and the Future

While the introduction of real balances represents a step forward in the development of the neoclassical theory of general equilibrium, it cannot be claimed to be of much empirical significance. And we must now face up to the question of why money yields utility—our justification for including it in the utility function of consumers. The fact is that money acts as a store of value not only for transactions purposes but also to satisfy the precautionary and speculative needs of consumers. These motives for holding money, which spring from uncertainty and from risk aversion, inescapably involve the future. And, in Keynes' view, these are the really significant functions of money: ". . . the importance of money essentially flows from it being a link between the present and the future." It is difficult to see how such functions can be adequately incorporated into an essentially static framework, in which consumers are assumed to be perfectly informed about the trading opportunities open to them within some finite time horizon.

So far as uncertainty is concerned, it may be argued that with perfect futures markets everywhere, there need be no incentive to hold money. Future expenditures and receipts can be planned today in the face of uncertainty through contracts for forward sales and purchases. If markets are perfect, money is not needed. However, such a comprehensive set of future markets does not exist, and even if it did they would probably not be perfect. The cost of organising them could be formidable and therefore it might cost society less in terms of real resources to use money.

In the absence of future markets, the theory of choice under uncertainty suggests why an asset with a zero rate of return like money should be held in preference to assets with prospective positive rates of return. The rate of return which is foregone in holding money may be regarded as an insurance premium against the possibility that the rate of return on the other assets may, in fact, turn out to be negative.

Money as a Medium of Exchange

The most noticeable function of money to most people is its convenience in facilitating transactions. In a monetised economy, we do not exchange directly the goods and services we supply with the goods and services produced by others. We exchange them for money, and then exchange the money for other goods and services we wish to acquire. Thus, in a monetised economy, exchange is a two-stage process, and money acts as the medium of exchange.

When the neoclassical economists proclaimed the "neutrality" of money, (i.e. the lack of impression which changes in monetary variables make upon the "real" sector of the economy), they were not of course denying the enormous changes in real output brought about by the transition from a barter economy to a monetised economy. Their views applied specifically within the context of an already monetised economy. This point is not in dispute. The neoclassical economists may be criticised, however, for continuing to treat a monetised economy as if it were, in fact, a barter economy from the point of view of exchange. In their systems, goods and services continue to exchange directly with each other, whereas in a monetised economy, where exchange is a two-stage process, all transactions are essentially speculative.[5] Whereas in a theoretical barter or pure exchange system,

[5] Unless proceeds of sales equal outlays on purchases by every transactor at every moment of time.

an essential feature is that one party must gain utility from an exchange system, and the other must not lose, this may not be true in an actual monetised economy. Should the second stage of the goods/money then money/goods exchange not materialise, the first stage by itself may result in a loss of utility by one party. The possibilities of disequilibrium in the system as a whole become quite evident when looked at from this point of view. Of course, the neoclassical economists were not so naïve as to ignore these facts altogether. Indeed, they did regard them as a source of possible short-run adjustment problems, which they discussed under the heading of the Theory of the Trade Cycle. But, until Keynes,[6] no one had supposed that the existence of money as a medium of exchange might be a source of long-run disequilibrium in a market economy.

Conclusions on Money

It is very doubtful whether money can usefully be incorporated in a static general equilibrium system, for the following reasons:

(i) The primary role of money in an economy involves intertemporal considerations, whereas most general equilibrium systems are single period.

(ii) Although some work has been done on uncertainty, general equilibrium theory has developed primarily within a framework of perfect information. The role of money, however, is largely influenced by uncertainty.

(iii) Money's role in the economy is therefore in problems of short-run adjustment, and disequilibrium behaviour. General equilibrium systems, on the other hand, are concerned with the nature of long-run equilibrium.

(iv) When money is introduced into a neoclassical system, in the form of real balances, the neutrality of money remains.[7]

Samuelson has suggested that money might usefully be regarded as part of the framework of economic activity. In this view, monetary institutions would be treated in much the same way as legal insti-

---

[6] Whether one believes that Keynes did suppose this depends on the interpretation placed on his writings (see chapter 8).

[7] This neutrality does not survive the introduction of more sophisticated monetary institutions such as credit markets and official monetary policy.

tutions. However, recent work by Hahn (1965) and others has tried to find reasons to justify the existence of money within a general equilibrium mode of analysis. This presupposes a reformulation of the concept of equilibrium which takes us beyond the scope of this book.

8 Keynes and the Neoclassical System

In the Introduction it was asserted that general equilibrium analysis was the most general form in which the theory of value was customarily expressed, and that simplification could take place in one of three directions: by turning into parameters most of the variables—a procedure which leads to the Marshallian partial equilibrium analysis; by simplification and specification of the functional relationships—a procedure which leads to some of the models considered in part III; and by aggregation—a procedure which leads to macroeconomic analysis. It is the third type of simplification which we follow in this chapter, and it is necessary since Keynes' criticisms of neoclassical economic theory were cast in a macroeconomic framework. Indeed, he was largely instrumental in establishing this type of analysis.

It is widely agreed that, in the General Theory, Keynes set out to show how a market economy could attain an equilibrium in which there was a negative excess demand for labour. It can also be agreed that the General Theory has had a dramatic impact upon economic thought and policy in market economy countries in the last three decades. Beyond this, there is very little agreement, since the General Theory contains a great number of theories and ideas, not always consistent, frequently vaguely formulated and therefore open to a variety of interpretations which economists have not been slow to provide.[1]

In this chapter, we shall present two polar interpretations of Keynes,

---

[1] And are still providing. See Leijonhufvud (1968), Hines (1971) and Clower (1965).

one representing a neoclassical view and the other an "ultra-Keynesian" view. But first we shall show how a macroeconomic system may be derived from a standard neoclassical system of general equilibrium.[2] We shall then use the derived system to illustrate a neoclassical view of Keynes' theory. In the following section, we present Patinkin's interpretation of Keynes, and conclude with some reflections on the compatibility of Keynes with neoclassical thinking.

General Equilibrium and Macroeconomic Analysis

Recall the simple general equilibrium system we postulated in the last chapter, equations (7.4), (7.5), and (7.7): it was composed of:

n Market Demand Equations

$$q_i = q_i(p_1, p_2, \ldots, p_n) \tag{8.1}$$

n Market Supply Equations

$$x_i = x_i(p_1, p_2, \ldots, p_n) \tag{8.2}$$

and
n Market Equilibrium Conditions

$$q_i = x_i \tag{8.3}$$

Notice that this system is already aggregated in the sense that the market demand and supply functions are aggregates of the individual demand and supply functions of all the consuming and producing units in the system. We now take the much more drastic step of *aggregating all goods into one.* In addition, we have one input, labour, and money. We shall denote labour and money variables with the subscripts l and m respectively. Thus our three-market system can now be written,

3 Market Demand Equations

$$q = q(p, p_l, p_m) \qquad \text{Demand for goods} \tag{8.4}$$

$$q_l = q_l(p, p_l, p_m) \qquad \text{Demand for labour} \tag{8.5}$$

$$q_m = q_m(p, p_l, p_m) \qquad \text{Demand for money} \tag{8.6}$$

[2] This section owes much to Hansen (1970) pp. 128-134.

3 Market Supply Equations

$$x = x(p, p_l, p_m) \qquad \text{Supply of goods} \qquad (8.7)$$

$$x_l = x_l(p, p_l, p_m) \qquad \text{Supply of labour} \qquad (8.8)$$

$$x_m = x_m(p, p_l, p_m) \qquad \text{Supply of money} \qquad (8.9)$$

3 Market Equilibrium Conditions

$$x = q \qquad \text{Equilibrium in goods market} \qquad (8.10)$$

$$x_l = q_l \qquad \text{Equilibrium in labour market} \qquad (8.11)$$

$$x_m = q_m \qquad \text{Equilibrium in money market} \qquad (8.12)$$

We next make specific assumptions about the forms and arguments of these relationships. Our choice of assumptions is directed by a desire to reflect those forms which figured in Keynes' writing, but we can reasonably continue to call our system "neoclassical", since nothing it contains is inconsistent with neoclassical thinking.[3] It will simplify the presentation if we deal with the equations of our system in reverse order, starting with (8.12).

(8.12)   No change

(8.11)   No change

(8.10)   The demand for the aggregate good is composed of demand for consumption and demand for investment. The familiar macro variables Y, C and I represent the *value* of output, consumption and investment respectively. $Y = pq$ in our notation. Thus (8.10) can be rewritten

$$Y/p = C/p + I/p \qquad (8.13)$$

(8.9)   The supply of money is determined exogenously. The macro-variable M is the *value* of the money supply, and when deflated by p gives the quantity of money in real terms

$$x_m = M/p \qquad (8.14)$$

(8.8)   The supply of labour is made a function of the wage/price ratio

---

[3] While our investment function has a neoclassical form, neoclassical economists generally worked within a static system in which the capital stock was taken as given. In this system, the need for an investment demand function did not arise.

$$x_l = x_l(p_l/p) \tag{8.15}$$

(8.7)   With a single input, and single output, the goods supply function is the simple production function

$$x = x(q_l) \tag{8.16}$$

(8.6)   Rewriting the demand for money in the specific form $q_m = q_m(p_m, p_l/p)$ is equivalent to writing $q_m = q_m(p_m, Y/p)$ since it can be shown that $Y/p = f(p_l/p)$.[4] Recognising p_m, the price which equilibrates the money market, as the rate of interest means that we are writing the demand for money in the familiar macro form as a function of two arguments, the rate of interest and the level of aggregate output

$$q_m = q_m(p_m, Y/p) \tag{8.17}$$

(8.5)   The demand function for labour is specified from the production equilibrium condition, $p_l/p = f'(q_l)$ i.e. the real wage = marginal product of labour. Thus

$$q_l = (f')^{-1}(p_l/p) \tag{8.18}$$

(8.4)   There are two demand functions for the good, one for consumption, the other investment. Writing C/p and I/p, respectively, for the *quantities* of these variables we can write the demand for investment as

$$I/p = I/p(p_m, p_l/p)$$

and for consumption as

$$C/p = C/p(p_m, p_l/p)$$

Making use again of the transformation, $Y/p = f(p_l/p)$, we can write these equations as

$$I/p = I/p(p_m, Y/p) \tag{8.19}$$

$$C/p = C/p(p_m, Y/p) \tag{8.20}$$

---

[4] Y = wages and profits. But wages = $p_l x_l = p_l \psi p_l/p$ (see 8.15). Profits = $px - p_l q_l$. From (8.16), $x = x(q_l)$ and from (8.18) $q_l = f'^{-1}(p_l/p)$. Thus we have

$$Y = p_l \psi(p_l/p) + pf[f'^{-1}(p_l/p)] - p_l f'^{-1}(p_l/p)$$

$$\therefore \quad Y = pF(p_l/p) \quad \therefore \quad Y/p = F(p_l/p)$$

Let us add the following definitional equation to bring the number of equations up to eleven:

$$Y/p = q \qquad (8.21)$$

There are eleven equations in our system, from (8.11) to (8.21), and eleven unknown variables: $C, I, q_l, q_m, x, x_l, x_m, p, p_l, p_m$ and Y. By slight rearrangement and substitution, but mainly by a change of notation, we can arrive at a system of equations thoroughly familiar to readers of macroeconomic texts. The changes in notation are writing r for p_m and M for x_m, w for p_l, N^D for q_l and N^S for x_l. Then we have:

1. $I/p = I/p(r, Y/p)$ from (8.19)
2. $C/p = C/p(r, Y/p)$ from (8.20)
3. $I = Y - C$ from (8.13)
4. $M/p = M/p(r, Y/p)$ from (8.12), (8.14) and (8.17)
5. $Y = pq$ from (8.21)
6. $q = \phi(N^D)$ from (8.10) and (8.16)
7. $w/p = \phi'(N^D)$ from (8.18)
8. $N^S = N^S(w/p)$ from (8.15)
9. $N^S = N^D$ from (8.11)

In this neoclassical macroeconomic system, there are nine unknown variables, M being assumed to be given exogenously.

A Neoclassical View of Keynes

The neoclassical macroeconomic model just derived enables us to depict very simply one possible interpretation of Keynes—the neoclassical one. It runs as follows:

If there is a permanent and significant degree of unemployment, then the labour market cannot be in equilibrium. Therefore, we must drop the last equation (no. 9), from our macroeconomic system. If we make w, the money wage rate, an exogenous variable, then we shall have a new "Keynesian" macrosystem of eight equations, which should have a determinate solution. But only by accident, if we happen to select the "right" value for w, will the demand for labour, N^D, turn out to be equal to the supply of labour, N^S. Clearly, if N^S is greater than N^D, it may be because too high a value of w is being selected. The implications of this view for policy are therefore that the cause of unemployment is that the money wage-rate has been fixed, (by trade-union pressure or perhaps by minimum wage legislation), above the level at which demand and supply would be equal. But even if a value for w is fixed, equilibrium in the market can still be restored by selecting an appropriate value for M, since demand and supply for labour are both functions of the *real* wage rate. Since a doubling of the money supply will lead to a doubling of the price level, it does not matter, in principle, whether the real wage rate is reduced by cutting the money wage rate, w, or increasing the money supply, M.

Since we are thinking in terms of general equilibrium systems, we must of course remember that a particular value selected for w, the price of labour, will not affect only the quantities supplied and demanded on the labour market, but will affect also the equilibrium values in both the other markets in the system. Conversely, values of non-labour market variables affect the equilibrium in the labour market. Thus, if we assume that our system has a unique equilibrium solution, and if we impose on one of the other variables a value other than its equilibrium value, then all three markets will be out of equilibrium. Thus observed unemployment, (a disequilibrium on the labour market), could be accounted for by some such disturbance elsewhere in the system. For example, if the rate of interest were prevented from falling to its equilibrium level by some device, this could prevent the system, including the labour market, from having an equilibrium solution. The Liquidity Trap is such a device. But Patinkin has shown that even the Liquidity Trap can be circumvented, if account is taken of the "real balance" effect. A sufficient reduction of money wages and thus prices, he argues, will have a positive effect on consumption expenditures by increasing the real value of money balances held by consumers, and thus will tend to restore a general equilibrium, including full employment of labour. Thus in this interpretation of Keynes, his system is reduced to that special case of the neoclassic system in which there is a downwards rigidity of money wage rates. It is evident that this is an interpretation that Keynes himself would have hesitated to accept, since, by his choice of title for his major work, he indicated that he believed that the neoclassical system was a special case of *his* General Theory.

If Keynes had spelled out the basic assumptions of his system, much of the confusion created by the General Theory might never have arisen. Instead, he criticised the neoclassical labour supply function, which he described as a "basic postulate" of "classical" theory, whereas it is in fact a derived function, as we have seen in chapter 1.

His frequent references to "unemployment equilibrium" are another major source of confusion. If one market is out of equilibrium in a general equilibrium system then, following Walras' Law, there must be at least one other market in the system which is also out of equilibrium. Yet it is clear from the General Theory that Keynes regarded all other markets as being in equilibrium. This, and the fact that the phrase "unemployment equilibrium" is something of a contradiction in terms have led some economists to argue that Keynes' "equilibrium" was not an equilibrium in the sense in which we have used it hitherto. This is the view of Patinkin, whose interpretation of Keynes we give below.

Then there is the question of time. It seems that Keynes was trying to describe a situation in which a market could be at rest, in some sense, for a prolonged period with significant levels of unemployment. Yet his system covers a period sufficiently short to be able to ignore the capacity-creating effects of investment.

Patinkin's Interpretation of Keynes

Patinkin's interpretation of the *General Theory*, which appears to be the most plausible[5] and constructive to date starts from the proposition that "involuntary unemployment can have no meaning within the confines of static equilibrium analysis". According to Patinkin the essential difference between Keynes' analysis and that of the neoclassical economists lies in the response of the system to a disturbance from an initial equilibrium. We are therefore back in the dynamic world of stability analysis which was sketched out in chapter 6. In the neoclassical view, a readjustment towards a new equilibrium or a restoration of the old takes place through the response of prices to a disequilibrium. This behaviour is of a type which can be represented by Walras' excess demand hypothesis. On the other hand, according to

[5] It must be conceded, however, that it is difficult to reconcile Patinkin's interpretation with the text of the General Theory. Grossman (1972) denies it provides any basis for the contention that "Keynes generally reversed the Marshallian rankings of relative price and quantity adjustment speeds." See Patinkin (1966).

Patinkin's interpretation, firms respond to a reduction in their expected
sales *not* by a reduction in the offer price, but by a reduction in the
volume of production and hence in the demand for labour. Likewise,
households respond to a reduction in their expected employment
opportunities by an acceptance of the reduced availability of employment. In this view, the economic system adapts by adjustments in
quantities of goods and factors supplied and demanded, while the
prices of goods and factors remain unchanged. Clearly this is a process
of adjustment which cannot be analysed within the traditional framework of analysis, not only because it requires a dynamic analysis, but
also because the traditional framework is constructed of functional
relations between quantities and prices, e.g. labour demand functions,
which are specifically held to be inoperative in this interpretation.

These two interpretations of Keynes can be contrasted in the
following way. The neoclassical interpretation follows the neoclassical
assumption of an infinite speed of adjustment of prices to any deviation
within the period concerned, while the speed of adjustment of
quantities is zero. Patinkin's interpretation presumes just the opposite:
a zero velocity of price adjustment and an infinite velocity of quantity
adjustment.

Patinkin's interpretation of Keynes is that he is questioning the
stability of the neoclassical general equilibrium system. If this is
correct, then Keynes' contribution might be seen as complementary
rather than hostile to the neoclassical analysis. The neoclassical
economists never denied that rigidities, friction, monetary and other
elements would create unemployment. Indeed, they developed the
theory of the trade cycle to deal with these phenomena. But they
would probably have agreed with Patinkin that the problems involved
are largely dynamic, and cannot usefully be dealt with in a static
system.

The Analysis of Disequilibrium

The interpretation of Keynes' criticisms as a discussion of the stability
properties of the neoclassical general equilibrium system is only mildly
comforting, in view of the well-known difficulties which stability
analysis encounters. These difficulties are augmented by the explicit
introduction of expectations, which played so large a part in Keynes
but which have scarcely been incorporated into the formal presentation
of his system. Consider, for example, Keynes' well-known proposition

that falling money wages may induce expectations of falling prices, and influence producers' behaviour accordingly. Arrow and Hahn pose the question: "How large must the expectation be in order to give the predicted instability? Unlike tâtonnement, the process takes place in real time, but how can one trace the consequences of disequilibrium behaviour at one moment on the behaviour of the economy in a subsequent moment?"

Without a dynamic model of the out-of-equilibrium behaviour of a market economy no general answer can be given to such a question. No such model exists but some recent work (Barro, 1971) has discussed the possible consequences of trading taking place out of equilibrium. It will be recalled that equilibrium prices are those which make it possible for every buyer and seller to buy and sell as much as he wants at those prices, so that every transactor's plans are consistent in the aggregate. If trading begins at disequilibrium or false prices, then the possibility arises that some transactor's plans will not be fulfilled. It will also be recalled from chapter 7 that in a monetary economy every act of exchange between two non-monetary commodities is necessarily indirect. The transactor first exchanges a commodity for money and then, if this plan is realised, he exchanges money for another commodity. Clearly, the second half of the transaction is contingent upon the successful completion of the first half. If the first plan is not realised, the second will not be. This consideration has led to a distinction being drawn between *notional* excess demands which reflect the real transformation possibilities of the economy and *effective* excess demands, which reflect the ability to pay in money. These two sets of excess demands are not equal when the system is out of equilibrium, since actual factor incomes are not equal to their equilibrium value. While it is the effective excess demands which constitute the relevant market signals, the sum of the value of all effective excess demands is not zero except in equilibrium, i.e. Walras' Law does not hold.

It may be asked whether, given some such state of disequilibrium, the system will necessarily converge over time to the familiar general equilibrium? No satisfactory answer to this question exists—it is simply the familiar problem of the stability of a neoclassical general equilibrium system, which we encountered earlier in chapter 6.

9 Welfare Economics—Basic Principles

Welfare economics is about alternative allocations of resources, i.e. alternative distributions of goods produced and consumed and factors used. It is to be contrasted with positive economics by virtue of the type of question it poses. In positive economics we ask questions like: "What will be the consequence for the price of x if we change the quantity of y demanded?", and go on to set up a model or theory to try to answer the question. If we arrive at an answer, the statement which embodies it may be said to be predictive. In welfare economics, on the other hand, we ask questions such as "is the allocation of resources A better than allocation B?" The model we set up to try to answer this type of question must include some criterion by which alternative allocations are to be judged. The statement which contains an answer to this type of question is described as *normative*. Despite the logical distinction between normative and predictive statements, the methods of both welfare economics and positive economics rely on the same models of the economic system, as we shall show in this and in the following two chapters.

Welfare economics is probably the most important theoretical application of the neoclassical general equilibrium analysis. It deals with alternative allocations of resources, which implies alternative distributions among more than one producer or consumer. Welfare economics cannot therefore be treated satisfactorily by partial equilibrium analysis. Attempts to do so involve decision rules whose significance and limitations can only be understood in the context of the general analysis from which they are derived.

Readers who followed the exposition of the neoclassical system in

chapter 5 will have noted that with a given set of parameters representing tastes and technology, and a given distribution of factor services
amongst households a unique set of relative prices and absolute quantities
of inputs and outputs was determined. This unique equilibrium solution
was the outcome of choices made by consumers and producers from
among many alternative feasible solutions. Welfare economics in the
widest sense is concerned with the choices which can be made from
among these alternative feasible solutions. In practice, much of the
discussion is confined to the subject of equilibrium solutions, for
reasons which will be made clear later in this chapter. But neoclassical
systems like (5.1) to (5.6) have a single equilibrium solution: how can
one speak about alternative equilibrium solutions? The answer,
formally, is that if we drop some of the sets of equations which
constitute our system we can get a number of alternative solutions
which will satisfy the remaining relationships. For example, if we
dropped both sets of market clearing equations (5.5) and (5.6), we
could obtain many solutions which are consistent with the remaining
four sets of equations But these solutions would not be equilibrium
solutions because all but one of them would be characterised by a
non-zero excess demand in two or more markets. And in welfare
economics, as in positive economics we are primarily interested in
equilibrium solutions.

What, in effect, happens in welfare economics is that the equations
which fix the distribution of factor services (and hence the distribution
of income), i.e. set (5.2), are dropped. Thus the possibility exists of a
very large number of different alternative solutions, each one satisfying
the usual remaining equilibrium conditions but each one corresponding
to a different distribution of income. A determinate solution can then
only be obtained by choosing amongst those alternatives according to
some new criterion. As we shall see, a number of criteria have been
proposed but it will help our exposition if we begin with the concept of
the social welfare function. If we can rank, according to some social
concensus, the wellbeing of different members of the community, then
this provides us, in principle, with a means of choosing amongst
alternative allocations of resources which leave different people better
or worse off.

The basic principles of welfare economics can be illustrated simply
with the aid of four figures.[1] These figures represent the resource

---

[1] The following passages draw heavily on Bator (1957).

allocation possibilities in an economy composed of two goods, two factors and two consumers.

We begin with the Edgeworth–Bowley box diagram, as in Fig. 9.1. The dimensions of the box represent the quantities of the two factors: this diagram is therefore appropriate for the assumption of fixed factor supplies. The sides of the box serve as axes for two sets of isoquants—one set representing the contours of the production function for good 1, with origin at O_1, the other for good 2 with origin at O_2. Points like A and C are points of tangency between

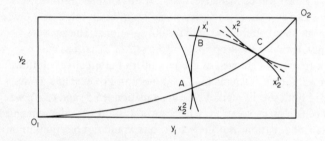

Fig. 9.1   The Edgeworth–Bowley production box

contours of the two functions. They are "efficient" points, compared to points like B. At B more of any one good can be produced by a reallocation of inputs without reducing the production level of the other. But at points like A and C, this is not possible. Such points as A and C are characterised by the equality of the rates of substitution, RSP, between the pair of inputs (y_1 and y_2) in the production of each good.[2] The line from O_1 to O_2 joining all such points is known as the *efficiency locus*. Even with constant returns to scale, this line generally has the concave or convex slope portrayed in Fig. 9.1. Only in the case

---

[2] The rate of substitution in production, RSP $y_1 y_2 \cdot x_1$, between two inputs y_1 and y_2 in the production of any good x_1 at any point is equal to the ratio of the marginal (physical) productivities of the two inputs at that point. In Fig. 9.1, the rate of substitution between the two inputs in the production of x_1 at A corresponds to the slope of the x_1 isoquant at A which is equal to the slope of the x_2 isoquant at the same point. In terms of the calculus

$$\frac{\partial x_1/\partial y_1}{\partial x_1/\partial y_2} = \frac{\partial x_2/\partial y_1}{\partial x_2/\partial y_2}$$

where the input proportions used in the production of each good are the same for any given input price ratio will the efficiency locus take the form of a diagonal straight line. To each point on the efficiency locus corresponds a pair of values of the output levels of the two goods, x_1 and x_2. When these values are plotted on axes representing quantities of each good, the resulting curve is described as the production possibility or production transformation curve. It generally has the shape illustrated in Fig. 9.2. The slope of this curve at any point

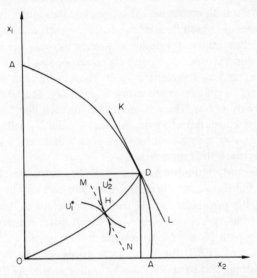

Fig. 9.2   Production transformation curve and trading box

represents the rate of transformation in production (RTP) at that point of x_1 into x_2. It shows how many additional units of x_1 can be produced at the margin by transferring inputs from the production of x_2 to the production of x_1, while maintaining the RSP equality condition of the previous diagram. It may be regarded as the marginal cost—in terms of x_2—of producing an additional unit of x_1, or, reciprocally, as the marginal cost in terms of x_1 of producing an additional unit of x_2.

   Any point on the curve, such as D, represents a particular combination of the quantities produced of each of the two goods x_1 and x_2. Another box diagram can be drawn whose dimensions correspond to these quantities by dropping from D lines parallel to the axes of Fig.

9.2. This box diagram is formally analogous to that of Fig. 9.1, but the interpretation is different. The contours which have their origins in the north-east and south-west corners of the box represent the ordinal preferences of each of the two consumers. The locus of points of tangency of the two indifference maps represents that locus of points within the box where any increase in the utility of consumer 1 implies a necessary reduction in the utility of consumer 2. So the line OD represents points of efficiency in consumption, characterised by the equality of the rate of substitution in consumption (RSC) between the pair of goods for both consumers. This is represented in the diagram by the equal slopes of the indifference curves of the two consumers at each point on OD. From the consumption efficiency locus we can read off the maximal combinations of U_1 and U_2 corresponding to the fixed amounts of x_1 and x_2 represented by D. These points can be plotted in a third diagram on axes representing U_1 and U_2, and labelled utility possibility curves. There is one curve for each point on the transformation curve, reflecting the fact that U_1 and U_2 will vary according to the way in which the given amounts of x_1 and x_2 are distributed between the consumers.

Now if the construction we have just described is repeated for every point on the transformation curve, the result will be a very large number of utility possibility curves. The outer envelope of these curves, the utility possibility frontier, is shown as the irregular line $AFEB$ in Fig. 9.3. Since both U_1 and U_2 are ordinal indexes we can infer nothing about the shape of $AFEB$ other than that it slopes downwards from left to right. It is important to understand the significance of $AFEB$. Each point represents the maximum level of U_1 which can be obtained by any feasible re-allocation of resources, whether in production and/or consumption, given some specified level of U_2, and *vice-versa*. The utility possibility frontier therefore represents diagramatically the concept of overall efficiency in welfare economics: that it be impossible by any shift in production and/or consumption to increase U_1 without reducing U_2.

There is a more direct way of deriving the utility possibility frontier from Fig. 9.2, a way which throws more light on its significance. Of all the points on the efficiency locus, OD, there is only one where the common slope of the indifference curves is equal to the slope of the transformation curve at D. At this point, let it be called H, the rate of substitution in consumption between the two goods, RSC, common to both consumers, is just equal to the rate of transformation in production between the two goods, RTP. If the values of U_1 and U_2 corresponding to H are read off from Fig. 9.2 and plotted in Fig. 9.3, they form a single point on the utility possibility frontier. Thus, corresponding to each point on the production transformation curve, there is one point on the utility possibility frontier. And each point on this efficiency frontier satisfies the condition that the subjective rate of substitution between the pair of goods which is common to both consumers is equal to the rate of transformation in production. This pairwise equality of rates of substitution and transformation is the hallmark of allocative efficiency in welfare economics.

In the next section we shall discuss the concept of efficiency and then compare efficiency conditions with the properties of neoclassical general equilibrium systems. Finally, we introduce the social welfare function to choose among all the points on the efficiency frontier, and thus obtain a determinate solution to our allocative problem. But first we recapitulate.

The purpose of welfare economics is to evaluate alternative allocations of resources. The traditional approach to the problem is to

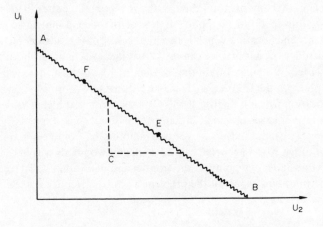

Fig. 9.3   The efficiency or utility possibility frontier

break it down into component problems–an efficiency problem and a distribution problem. This is illustrated in Fig. 9.3. The two axes measure, respectively, the utilities of the two individuals or households who compose the society. The irregular line AB represents the efficiency frontier (the utility possibility frontier), of the society. This is generated in the following way. Given fixed factor supplies, a unique transformation function for the society may be plotted in commodity space. Each point on this function defines an alternative commodity combination that can be efficiently attained with the available factor supplies. Each commodity combination may be distributed between the consumers in a number of alternative ways. Thus a utility possibility curve may be drawn for every single point on the transformation function, corresponding to the fact that the single commodity combination will give rise to a distribution of utilities according to the different ways in which the combination is distributed. The efficiency frontier is then the outer envelope of the set of utility possibility curves yielded by every point on the transformation curve. This frontier shows the maximum pairs of utility levels that could be achieved by varying both the combination of goods produced and their distribution. It embodies the concept of efficiency defined by the equality of the RTP between the pairs of goods and the common RSC. A very large number of allocations, including those represented by points E and F as well as A and B, satisfy this condition. Nor can we even claim that any point on the frontier is necessarily better than any point within it. From the point of view of the second individual, F represents an allocation which leaves him worse off (i.e. a lower level of U_2) than does C. All that we can say is that if society is at an allocation represented by a point within the frontier, such as C, then there will be *some* point on the frontier, such as E, northeast of C, corresponding to an allocation which is "better than" C, in the sense that higher values of *both* utility indexes obtain at E than at C. Without some explicit criterion we cannot judge whether one point on the frontier is better than another. Nor, in general, can we compare two points within the frontier nor even one point on the frontier and one within it. To resolve this distributional aspect of the problem we must introduce a social welfare function.

The Social Welfare Function

The role of the social welfare function is to enable choices to be made between alternative allocations which leave at least one individual worse off. Not only does it select the optimum E, from all of the efficient

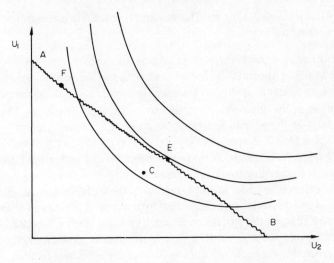

Fig. 9.4   The efficiency frontier with contours of the social welfare function

allocations represented by points on *AFEB* it also permits the comparison of points within the frontier as well (Fig. 9.4).

The formal properties which must be satisfied by a social welfare function may be summarised as follows:

(1) It is a function of the utility indexes of the individuals who compose the society. No other variables enter as arguments, hence it may be written as $W = W(U_1, U_2, \ldots U_s)$.

(2) It is a single valued function of its arguments, and a given level of welfare together with given levels of utility for all but one individual implies a unique level for that individual's utility index.

(3) $\partial W/\partial U_i > 0$, for all i. Diagramatically, this means that as we move north east from any point we cross contours of increasing value. The contours cannot be vertical or horizontal over any range, nor can they meet or cross otherwise their curvature is just as arbitrary as the curvature of the efficiency frontier, since the utility indices are ordinal.

(4) $\partial U_i/\partial U_j < 0$, for $i \neq j$. This requires that welfare contours be downward sloping.

Any function which satisfies these criteria will perform satisfactorily its role. In Fig. 9.4, point E is identified to be the welfare optimum, and thus a particular allocation of resources in production and consumption is chosen as the one which maximises the welfare of the society. The contours of the welfare function also reveal that society prefers allocation C to F, despite the fact that F is on the efficiency frontier while C is not. Likewise, all other allocations on and within the frontier are ranked according to social preference.

We can now see how the introduction of the social welfare function permits us to determine the level and distribution of inputs and outputs corresponding to the welfare optimum. The social welfare function identifies one point, E, on the efficiency frontier as representing the welfare optimum. From our construction of the efficiency frontier, recall that to each point on $AFEB$ there corresponds just one point on the production transformation curve AA in Fig. 9.2. Suppose that point is D. Then find the point, H, on the curve OD where the values of U_1 and U_2 correspond to those at E in Fig. 9.4. The common slopes of the indifference curves at H equal the slope of the transformation curve at D. Point D fixes the total quantities of x_1 and x_2 produced and H fixes the distribution of these goods between the two consumers. Finally we know from the construction of the production transformation curve AA that every point on it corresponds to just one point on the production efficiency locus $O_1 O_2$ in Fig. 9.1. Suppose the point on O_1 O_2 corresponding to D on AA is C. Then C fixes the values of the remaining variables: the allocation of the two factor inputs y_1 and y_2 in the production of the two goods. Thus the optimal allocation of resources is determined.

But all this is completely formal. How is the social welfare function actually to be determined? In a dictatorship, it presumably reflects the preferences of the ruling group, but in a democratic society how can a social welfare function be constructed? Is there any procedure by which the preferences of individual members of society could be reflected in a social welfare function? This was the question to which Arrow (1951) addressed himself. Specifically, he asked whether any method was possible, which would satisfy five axioms, which in his judgement were minimally acceptable ones, of translating individual into social preferences.

Arrow's Five Axioms

The five axioms proposed by Arrow were as follows:

1. *Complete Ordering*

It must be possible for all social states to be ordered by the relation "is preferred to or is indifferent to", and this ordering must satisfy similar conditions of completeness, reflexitivity, and transitivity observed by individual preferences in the formation of individual utility functions.

2. *Responsiveness to Individual Preferences*

If any given set of individual preferences is such that A is then said to be socially preferred to B, and if individual preferences change so that at least one individual raises A to a higher rank, and none lowers A in rank, then A must remain socially preferred to B. The significance of this axiom is that it rules out discrimination by society against any minority group.

3. *Nonimposition*

Social preferences cannot be imposed independently of individual preferences. If no individual prefers B to A, and at least one prefers A to B, then society must prefer A to B.

4. *Nondictatorship*

Social preferences must not reflect solely the preferences of any single individual.

5. *Independence of Irrelevant Alternatives*

The most preferred state must be independent of the existence of other alternatives. If society prefers A to B and B to C, then if C is no longer available, society must not prefer B to A.

Arrow then went on to prove that it is not possible to construct social preferences from well-behaved individual preferences in any way which would satisfy these five simple principles simultaneously. This conclusion indicates that if choices are to be made between alternative allocations, we must rely on a less ambitious criterion than a social welfare function.

Efficiency Conditions

In the last section, we illustrated the concept of efficiency in the special case of two goods, two consumers, and fixed supplies of two factors. We now must generalise. Efficiency can be defined at two levels: (i) efficiency in production or consumption, and (ii) overall efficiency in the economy as a whole. Efficiency in consumption (including leisure and other consumed primary inputs) is realised if every possible reallocation of a given bundle of goods amongst other consumers results in the reduction of the utility of at least one. This condition will be satisfied if, for each consumer, the rate of substitution in consumption between any given pair of goods is the same. To see that this is so it is only necessary to consider an example of a pair of goods and two consumers for which the equality does not hold. If the subjective rate at which consumer A is willing to substitute beer for cigarettes is 10 cans of beer for 100 cigarettes while consumer B's rate of substitution is 10 cans of beer for 200 cigarettes, then an exchange between them at the rate of, say, 1 can for 15 cigarettes would leave both better off. The possibility of improvement in the utility of at least one will continue to exist so long as any discrepancy exists between the rates at which they subjectively substitute between some given pair of goods.

Efficiency in production is said to exist if no re-allocation of inputs within commodity production is possible without a lesser amount of some commodity being produced, i.e. it is not possible to produce more of any one good without producing less of any other good. This condition is fulfilled if the rate of substitution between any given pair of inputs is the same in the production of every commodity in which the pair of inputs are used. The reader should be able to construct for himself an example, in the style of the previous paragraph, to show that the pairwise equality of rates of substitution in production will satisfy the production efficiency condition.

Overall efficiency, i.e. efficiency in the whole economic system, exists when no possible reallocation of commodities or inputs either within or between production and consumption could make one consumer better off without leaving at least one other worse off. Such an allocation is said to be efficient in the sense of Pareto,[3] and is described by the simultaneous satisfaction of the following three conditions:

(i) For any pair of goods in the system, the subjective rate of substitution common to all consumers must be equal to the rate of transformation in production common to all firms.

(ii) For any pair of inputs, the common subjective rate at which suppliers substitute between them must be equal to the common rate of substitution in production.

(iii) For any pair consisting of one commodity and one input, the subjective rate of substitution must be equal to the common rate of transformation.[4]

Thus it is the existence in an economic system of a common set of transformation and substitution ratios which is the essence of the notion of allocative efficiency. It is vital to realise that transformation and substitution ratios do exist in every economic system, regardless of whether or not a price system, (i.e. a set of exchange ratios), exists. The realisation of some degree of allocative efficiency is thought to be an important objective of a well-designed price system, whether it be established through a set of markets, by computer, by decree, or by any other means. The extent to which the exchange ratios it prescribes correspond to the underlying substitution and transformation ratios of the economy constitutes a measure of its success.

[3] Since a very large number of alternative allocations may satisfy these conditions, the description "Pareto-optimal", which is sometimes used to refer to an efficient allocation, is misleading and should be avoided. Note that conditions (ii) and (iii) cannot be applied to our geometric example of the last section. These conditions presume that inputs are variable in supply, whereas we took them to be fixed in supply.

[4] For example, the common subjective rate at which consumers are willing to substitute 1 hour of leisure for one pair of shoes should be equal to the rate at which 1 hour of labour is transformed into shoes (i.e. the marginal physical product of labour in the production of shoes).

Efficiency and Equilibrium

The three efficiency conditions just laid down constitute the necessary conditions for a welfare optimum. But unless the second-order or sufficient conditions are simultaneously realised, then adherence to the efficiency conditions may lead to an allocation far removed from an optimum. What are the second-order conditions for a welfare optimum? As in the case of the positive neoclassical model, they are concerned with the curvature (i.e. rate of change of slope), of the production and preference functions in the system. Unless these are the "right shape", (e.g. convex to the origin in the case of indifference curves and production function isoquants and concave to the origin in the case of the production transformation curve), then a particular allocation which satisfies the efficiency conditions—either overall or at the production or consumption level—may correspond to a minimum rather than a maximum value of the appropriate function. This point is discussed and illustrated in chapter 10, p. 106, below. It should also be noted that our efficiency conditions are necessary conditions for a welfare optimum only when the social welfare function is of the type we have specified. If, for example, the utility functions of some individuals entered another social welfare function negatively (e.g. a dictator possessed of a hatred of one social group), then the efficiency conditions would not be necessary conditions for the realisation of that welfare optimum.

It can be shown very easily that equilibrium solutions to neoclassical systems satisfy the conditions for allocative efficiency which have just been laid down. Let us consider, for instance, the efficiency condition for the consumption of commodities, which require that the rate of substitution between any pair of goods should be the same for all households. Recall that in establishing the theory of consumption (p. 5), the same first order conditions from which we derive the consumer's demand function also yielded the result that the consumer's utility would be maximised when, for any pair of commodities, his subjective rate of substitution was equal to their price ratio, i.e.

$$- \frac{\partial q_{ik}}{\partial q_{jk}} = \frac{p_j}{p_i}$$

But one characteristic of a neoclassical equilibrium is a unique set of prices of commodities. Hence the rate of substitution between pairs of goods must be the same for *all* households. Similar reasoning can be used to establish the equivalence of neoclassical equilibrium and efficiency conditions in the production sector and overall. In the case of the production sector, the neoclassical assumptions require that each producer should pay the same price for a given type of input, and receive the same price for a given type of output. Once again, the existence of a common price set is the essence of the welfare efficiency conditions.

Thus a neoclassical equilibrium will correspond, in the terms of our diagram, to some point on the efficiency frontier. But which point will it be? Clearly, the location of the point will be determined by the distribution of income, which in turn will depend on the distribution of ownership of factor services. Only by chance will this point coincide with the welfare optimum denoted by E in Figs 9.3 and 9.4. However, it is possible, in theory, to move from the neoclassical equilibrium, let us say it is point F, to E by suitable lump-sum transfers of income. In this way, it is possible to think of the realisation of a welfare optimum as having an efficiency component and a distributional component.

Therefore we may conclude that a neoclassical equilibrium is a necessary but not a sufficient condition for a welfare optimum. Since a neoclassical equilibrium is neutral with respect to a number of alternative institutional arrangements, it is wrong to suppose that a system of perfectly competitive markets is either necessary or sufficient for a welfare optimum.

One important ingredient of our earlier neoclassical equilibrium analysis appears to be missing from welfare optimisation: in the latter analysis, there is no mention of prices. Actually, they are implicit in the solution. We know from the theory of the firm that production at minimum cost takes place when the rate of substitution between two inputs (RSP) is just equal to their price ratio. The implicit or "shadow" input price ratio is accordingly represented by the slope of the dotted line through C in Fig. 9.1. Likewise, the slope of the parallel lines KL and MN in Fig. 9.2 denoting the common RSC = RTP between the two goods represents their price ratio which is implied by the optimal solution. The third independent price ratio in the system, that relating input prices and output prices, is not directly represented in the diagrams but can be derived from them. The phenomenon of implicit or shadow prices is extremely significant: it shows that any allocation of resources inescapably implies a set of prices. In Part III, we shall see that the converse is also true: any set of equilibrium prices implies a particular set of quantities of goods produced and consumed. It may be asked, how are these shadow prices related to the set of prices in a corresponding neoclassical general equilibrium? The answer is that if decisions are made in response to these prices either by decentralised utility and profit maximisers or by a centralised computer programme, and all the usual assumptions hold, the result will be that configuration of inputs, outputs and their distribution which characterises the welfare optimum.

Compensation Criteria

Some attempts have been made to rank alternative allocations without recourse to distributional considerations. Not only is the social welfare function ruled out, so are any interpersonal comparisons of utility. Thus the allocations to be ranked, variously described in the literature as "states" or "positions", or even "policies" are in effect alternative collections of produced goods. Each collection may be represented, in the terms of our diagrams, by a single utility possibility curve, each point on the curve representing a different distribution between two consumers of the given collection of goods.

Kaldor proposed in 1939 that one collection of goods, Q, should be considered better than another R, if those who gained from the change from R to Q could afford to compensate fully the losers by the change, and still themselves be better-off. This criterion is illustrated in Fig. 9.5. In the figure, the collection of goods Q is represented by the utility possibility curve QQ^1, while the collection R is represented by RR^1. If the initial distribution of R leaves both consumers at r_1 then a change

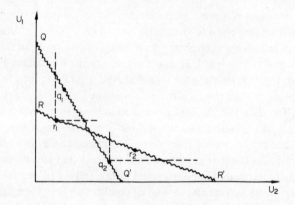

Fig. 9.5   The inconsistency of Kaldor's compensation criterion

to Q would be a welfare improvement in Kaldor's sense, since collection Q *could* be distributed in the manner represented by q_1, which leaves each consumer better-off than he was at r_1.

Two years later Scitovsky pointed out that Kaldor's criterion could lead to inconsistency; it could not only show that Q was preferred to R, but also that R was preferred to Q. Suppose that, in accordance with the initial test society has moved to Q. If the distribution of Q is represented by q_2 then R must be an improvement on Q in Kaldor's sense, since both consumers are better-off at r_2 than they are at q_2. Scitovsky then proposed that one collection of goods should be judged "better" than another in a welfare sense only if Kaldor's test worked in *both* directions.

The principal objection to such criteria is that the compensation remains purely hypothetical. Thus a potential improvement, in Kaldor's or Scitovsky's sense, might be associated with an actual outcome in which one individual was made very much worse off (i.e. was not actually compensated).

Other Criteria

We know, as a matter of experience, that changes in economic policy brings gains to some sections of the community and losses to others. They are not generally followed by redistributive measures designed to give effect to the compensation principle. Consequently, the distribution between *actual* and *hypothetical* compensation is a very real one and not merely academic. Perhaps, then, we should adopt as our welfare criterion the requirement that any change of policy must actually leave *no-one* worse-off than before. There are two main objections to this as a possible welfare criterion.

First, it is unrealistic. Although we should be careful to bear in mind that we are theorising, and not devising operational criteria, nevertheless there is not much point in devising a test which most major policy proposals will fail to pass.

The second objection to the criterion of actual compensation, which applies equally to all compensation criteria, is that it ignores distributional considerations. It is reasonable to suppose that a modern democratic society may have a consensus about the direction of desirable changes in the distribution of income. Mishan therefore argues that we should adopt a dual welfare criterion. According to this, an improvement in welfare would be defined to occur if (a) a change led to a new position in which all were at least no worse off, and (b) some movement in the direction of greater equality of income distribution was realised. The latter point reflects Mishan's judgement that this reflects the preferences of modern democratic societies, while the former aspect makes the criterion somewhat restricted in scope, as he recognises. Indeed the illustration he offers of the type of change which might pass his test is that of an "unanticipated technical innovation".[5]

Appendix

In this chapter we have presented the basic principles of welfare economics using familiar diagrammatic methods. The connection between welfare and positive economics may however be made clearer if we formulate the welfare maximisation problem algebraically, using an example with two goods, two consumers and fixed factor supplies.

Writing the utility functions of the two consumers as

$$U_1 = U_1(q_{11}, q_{21}) \tag{9.A1}$$

and

$$U_2 = U_2(q_{12}, q_{22}) \tag{9.A2}$$

then the social welfare function may be written

$$W = W(U_1, U_2) \tag{9.A3}$$

Welfare maximisation may then be seen as the maximisation of (9.A3) subject to the constraints imposed by the availability of the two goods. With fixed factor supplies the production function may be written in implicit form as $\phi(q_{11} + q_{12}, q_{21} + q_{22}) = 0$. Forming the expression

$$Z = W[U_1(q_{11}, q_{21}), U_2(q_{12}, q_{22})]$$
$$+ \lambda\phi(q_{11} + q_{12}, q_{21} + q_{22}) \tag{9.A4}$$

and setting the partial derivatives to zero, we obtain the first order conditions for constrained welfare maximisation. This procedure is analagous to identifying a welfare optimum in a two dimensional diagram where the production possibility curve is tangent to one of the contours of a community indifference function. Writing W_i as the ith partial derivative of the welfare function, and ϕ_i as the ith partial deriva-

[5] Mishan (1969) p. 74.

tive of the production function, then the five equations which can be
derived from (9.A4) are as follows:

$$\frac{\partial Z}{\partial q_{11}} = W_1 \frac{\partial U_1}{\partial q_{11}} + \lambda \phi_1 = 0$$

$$\frac{\partial Z}{\partial q_{21}} = W_1 \frac{\partial U_1}{\partial q_{21}} + \lambda \phi_2 = 0$$

$$\frac{\partial Z}{\partial q_{12}} = W_2 \frac{\partial U_2}{\partial q_{12}} + \lambda \phi_1 = 0 \qquad (9.A5)$$

$$\frac{\partial Z}{\partial q_{22}} = W_2 \frac{\partial U_2}{\partial q_{22}} + \lambda \phi_2 = 0$$

$$\frac{\partial Z}{\partial \lambda} = \phi(q_{11} + q_{12}, q_{21} + q_{22}) = 0$$

By moving the second term in each equation to the right hand side, and
then dividing the first equation by the second, and the third equation
by the fourth, we obtain

$$\frac{\partial U_1/\partial q_{11}}{\partial U_1/\partial q_{21}} = \frac{\phi_1}{\phi_2} = \frac{\partial U_2/\partial q_{12}}{\partial U_2/\partial q_{22}} \qquad (9.A6)$$

This statement says that the rate of substitution in consumption
between the two commodities is the same for both consumers and is
equal to the rate of transformation in production, ϕ_1/ϕ_2.

The five equations in (9.A5) form a system of simultaneous
equations which may be solved for the five variables q_{11}, q_{21}, q_{12},
q_{22}, and λ. Assuming that the second order conditions are also satisfied, this solution will represent the welfare optimum. How does this
normative solution compare with the solution to a "positive" general
equilibrium analysis, as illustrated by the two sector example on p. 41.
The first apparent difference is that the solution to the normative
analysis gives no indication of the quantities of factor services used in
the production of each good, nor does it contain any price variables. It
is true that the factor quantities do not appear explicitly in the solution
to (9.A5) but they may easily be calculated from the implicit production function, knowing the total quantities of each factor and the
quantities of each good produced. Likewise a set of prices is implicit in
the solution to (9.A5). There are four unknown prices, p_1, p_2, r_1 and

r_2. Recognising that we can only hope to solve for relative prices, we can put $r_1 = 1$, and try to solve for the remaining three prices. We need three additional equations to do this. We know that in the optimal solution the price ratio of the pair of goods must be equal to the rate of transformation in production, therefore we can write (i) $p_1/p_2 = \phi_2/\phi_1$. We also know that efficiency requires that inputs be used in production up to the point where the marginal product times the price of the extra output just equals the input price, i.e. (ii) $p_1 = \phi_1 r_1$ and (iii) total cost must equal total revenue so that $r_1 y_1 + r_2 y_2 = p_1(q_{11} + q_{12}) + p_2(q_{21} + q_{22})$. These three equations should suffice to solve for the three unknown relative price ratios which are implicit in the solution.

Supposing that in both positive and normative models, the initial factor supplies, consumers preferences and production functions were the same would the solutions to the two problems be identical? In general the answer is no, since in the positive case the solution is also influenced by the distribution of the ownership of factors. This influence is replaced in the case of the normative model by the social welfare function. Only by chance would the two solutions coincide. Notice that because of our simplifying assumption in both models that factor supplies are fixed, the distribution of income does not affect the supply of factors. However, in the general case, differences in the distribution of income, other parameters remaining the same, would be associated with differences in the supply of factors.

10 Welfare Economics—
Complications and Conclusions

The welfare criteria discussed in the last chapter were unsatisfactory for different reasons. The theoretical and practical difficulties of constructing an acceptable social welfare function appear to be insuperable. Compensation criteria may be acceptable if compensation is actually paid, but we know that this will seldom happen. What prescriptions then does neoclassical welfare economics have to offer economic policy-makers in choosing between different allocations?

Let us assume that there is some identifiable welfare optimum, located by political choice at some point such as E on the efficiency frontier. Then the neoclassical strategy may be summarised in two stages:

(1) First establish a uniform set of exchange ratios which correspond to the transformation and substitution ratios existing in the economy. (In the terms of partial equilibrium analysis, this is equivalent to setting prices equal to marginal costs.) This is sufficient, subject to the usual qualifications, to move the economy onto its efficiency frontier.
(2) Second, move along the efficiency frontier to the desired point by a method of income redistribution which will leave undisturbed the equality of exchange, transformation, and substitution ratios.

In chapter 9 we showed that realisation of a neoclassical equilibrium would bring us to the efficiency frontier. But the existence of such an equilibrium is founded on certain assumptions which we must now examine more closely. Certain real-world phenomena would appear to invalidate some of these assumptions.

Deviations between Private and Social Costs

Should some discrepancy arise between the true opportunity cost to society of obtaining an additional unit of any good, and the money cost to which the decision-maker responds, then the resulting allocation will be less than completely efficient and the economy will be operating within its efficiency frontier.

Monopolies, externalities, and taxes may all[1] be regarded as examples of a discrepancy existing between the rate of substitution in consumption and the rate of transformation in production. This is illustrated in Fig. 10.1. The figure shows the production transformation

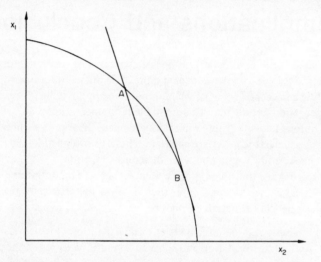

Fig. 10.1   Deviation between private and social cost

curve for an economy in which there are two goods. The slope of the curve at any point represents society's true rate of transformation at that point. The slope of the straight lines through A and B represents the perceived private rate of substitution.

---

[1] In this context, 'monopolies' refer to all forms of imperfect competition except bilateral and perfectly discriminating monopoly, externalities means all forms of non-market interdependence between consumers and/or producers, while 'taxes' includes all non lump-sum taxes. A lump-sum tax is one which does not cause producers or consumers to alter their buying or selling decisions. Taxes on factor incomes are not lump-sum taxes unless factor supplies are assumed to be perfectly inelastic (see p. 107).

In the case of monopoly, x_2 is the good produced by the mono-polised sector. Production takes place at A where less x_2 is produced than at B and the ratio of prices, p_2/p_1 is higher than the ratio of money marginal costs, reflected in the slope of the curve at A. The abolition of the monopoly would lead to a shift of production from A to B accompanied by an alteration in the relative price ratio. At B the potential rate of transformation coincides with that perceived by individual producers.

In the case of taxation, suppose there is an *ad valorem* tax on the consumption of good 2. Production and consumption take place at A, where the market price ratio (equal to the consumer's rate of substi-tution) is represented by the slope of the straight line, and where the slope of the curve again represents the rate of transformation in production. Removal of the tax alters the price ratio and shifts pro-duction and demand to B.

In the case of external economies, good 2 is again the good which generates benefits in production which are not captured by its producers. This accounts for the discrepancy between the price ratio and the rate of transformation. A subsidy on the production of x_2 will bring the price ratio into line with the rate of transformation, and shift production from A to B.

Correction of the discrepancy will in each case lead to a "better" allocation of resources, in the familiar sense of an increase in potential welfare or potential social dividend. Redistribution of all or part of this dividend through a set of lump-sum taxes and transfers should make it possible, in principle, for this welfare gain to be realised, in the sense that all parties are at least as well off as they were before the correc-tions were made. Thus deviations between private and social costs, *so long as they are open to correction*, present no insuperable theoretical difficulties. If, however, such deviations are ineradicable they give rise to "second-best" problems.

Public Goods

A public good can be most simply defined as one for which the opportunity cost of consumption is zero. While, like a private good, it will have positive production costs, it is distinguished by the charac-teristic that its consumption by one person does not diminish its availability to other consumers. Therefore, if we wish to take account of public goods in our analysis, we must modify our statement of the efficiency conditions.

Frequently associated with public goods is the characteristic that in some cases producers may not be able to practise exclusion, while in other cases consumers may not be able to practise exclusion. This second characteristic does not disturb the efficiency conditions, but it does have implications for the feasibility of the operation of a market price mechanism.

It will be recalled that, in the case of private goods, efficiency conditions were formulated in terms of the pairwise equality of rates of substitution and transformation between goods. If one of the pair of goods is a public good then we must reformulate the efficiency conditions to take account of the property that consumption of a unit of the public good by one consumer does not necessarily preclude consumption of the same unit by other consumers. For example, if the pair of goods is defence services (a public good), and automobiles (a private good), the appropriate efficiency condition requires the equality of the rate of transformation in production and the *sum* of the rates of substitution between the two goods over *all* the consumers.[2] The reformulation of the efficiency conditions, however, requires no more than summation on one or both sides to the relevant equality[3]: no change of principle is involved.

If the public good is of the kind that its producers cannot exclude any potential users (e.g. defence services, broadcasting, most kinds of information) then they cannot charge a price for its use. In such cases, even when the appropriate efficiency conditions are fulfilled, a market

[2] As Winch (1971) points out, in an excellent chapter on this subject, many of the individuals may have negative rates of substitution. In the case of such a public good as pollution, the aggregate consumers' rates of substitution will probably be negative. But so will the corresponding rate of transformation, since it will require the use of resources to prevent the production of the good (or the "bad" as it may more appropriately be entitled).

[3] Specifically, the overall efficiency condition involving one public good and one private good may be formulated as follows: If $RSC_{x_1 \cdot x_2}$ is the rate of substitution for each consumer s between a public good x_1 and a private good x_2, then the efficiency condition can be rewritten as

$$\sum_s RSC_{x_1 \cdot x_2} = RTP_{x_1 \cdot x_2}$$

price system cannot be relied upon to ensure production of the good. If on the other hand, producers can practise exclusion, and the public good is marketable, a market price system may fail to satisfy the efficiency conditions. Since the opportunity cost of providing units of the good to additional consumers is zero, it will be inefficient to charge any price other than zero. To charge a non zero price for a public good may be to deprive the marginal consumer of a benefit which costs society nothing.

Two classic examples of the problem of pricing of public goods are (a) Information, and (b) the service of a bridge operating at less than capacity. (Once the bridge is operating at full capacity, the service it provides ceases to be a public good.) Both commodities satisfy the definition of a public good. In both cases the producer may practise exclusion, and charge a price for each unit of the commodity. In the case of information, this can be done by copyright or patent, while in the case of a bridge a toll may be charged on each crossing. However charging a uniform price per unit will almost certainly violate efficiency conditions, since it may deter the marginal consumer from availing himself of a unit of a good which costs society nothing to provide. Making the services freely available raises the question of how the generators of information and producers of bridges are to be remunerated, since it can be assumed that, like other commodities, their supply will be a function of price received. One solution would be to accept the loss implied by violation of the efficiency conditions, and to justify a uniform non-zero price on distributional grounds. The theoretically preferred solution would be to levy revenue from the beneficiaries (the consumers of the public good) in such a way that there would be no disincentive to consumption of the good. This is an argument in favour of either, (a) lump-sum taxes, or (b) allowing the producer of the public good to act as a perfectly discriminating monopolist. Whichever policy is preferred would depend in theory on distributional considerations, and in practice, on feasibility.

An externality may be viewed as one member of a pair of joint products which is a public good.[4] If the producer can practise exclusion, then the possibility exists of the price being corrected accordingly, as was suggested above. However, if exclusion is not possible, and external costs and/or benefits cannot be internalised, then market prices will give the "wrong" signals, and efficiency conditions will not be fulfilled. It has been suggested by Mishan that

[4] A little reflection will suggest that all goods may be regarded in a sense as possessing externalities.

uncorrected externalities provide a major reason for the unsatisfactory nature of measured GNP as an indicator of society's welfare.

Indivisibilities

Neoclassical analysis is based upon the supposition that all functions and variables are continuous. Thus consumers and producers may be supposed to be able continuously to adjust their sales and purchases so that equality of rates of substitution and transformation may always be established.

But often actual decisions may be of a "lumpy" or "all or nothing" character. For example, work is offered in lumps made up of 8-hour shifts or 5-day weeks. A consumer purchases only one car or one house at a time. In the former case, the individual may not be able to adjust the number of hours worked so as precisely to equalise his preferred rate of substitution between leisure and income with the wage rate. In the latter case, equilisation of the rate of substitution between two goods and their price ratio may be impossible for similar reasons. Although in neither case are the efficiency conditions exactly satisfied, they can be approximated.

More serious problems arise when the indivisibility is large, not just with respect to one individual, but with respect to the total market. For example, the capacity of one power station or one steel mill in an under-developed country may be so large in relation to the market that the demand curve for its output is less than perfectly elastic. This introduces an inescapable degree of arbitrariness into the valuation of its benefits. The problem may be further complicated by the pheno- menon of average costs decreasing over the relevant range of output as a result of the large fixed costs associated with such an indivisibility. Pricing of the output in accordance with the efficiency conditions will, in such circumstances, fail to realise revenue sufficient to cover total costs. The solution lies in distinguishing the decision of pricing the output of the indivisible good from the decision whether or not the indivisible good should be put in place (i.e. the investment decision). The investment decision depends on whether the total social benefit is greater or less than the total cost. The pricing decision should be based on the efficiency conditions. Any shortfall between the resulting revenue and the total cost of the project (assuming it to have been judged worthwhile), should be financed by some lump-sum tax raised according to whatever distributive principle is preferred.

Indivisibility of some inputs frequently accounts for the phenomenon of increasing returns to the other, variable, inputs over some
range of output of a commodity. The classic example here is the service
provided by a transport system (railway, bus service, or airline). The
addition of units of equipment (carriages, buses, aircraft) may be
followed by a range of outputs exhibiting increasing returns until the
equipment is fully utilised. The problem of increasing returns to scale
is part of the problem of nonconvexity in economics.

Nonconvexity

Convexity is an important concept in economic analysis which concerns
the curvature or rate-of-change-of slope of functions. However, it
should on no account be confused with curvature that appears convex
to the origin. We shall discuss two examples of convexity which should
make this clear. But let us begin with a definition: convexity obtains if
a straight line connecting any two feasible points does not anywhere
pass outside the set of feasible points.

Consider first of all the isoquants of a production function as
illustrated in Fig. 9.1. They are drawn there in their normal shape, i.e.
convex to the origin. This representation is in line with the definition of
convexity just given. The feasible input combinations which can
produce the output quantity indicated by the isoquant lie north-east of
the contour line, and no straight line joining these points passes outside
the set (see Fig. 10.2(i)). A different situation is shown in Fig. 10.2(ii),
where a straight line joining some points does pass outside the set.
Thus the set of points is said to be non convex. To show that nonconvexity is not confined to functions non-convex to the origin,
consider a second example of nonconvexity: increasing returns to scale.
It will be recalled that increasing returns to scale can be represented on
a production isoquant diagram by isoquants that are closer together as
one moves outward along any straight line from the origin. This simply
reflects the essential property of increasing returns to scale that
doubling the output requires less than double the inputs. How is this
property, supposing it to be represented in the construction of a
production box diagram such as Fig. 9.1 reflected in the shape of the
production transformation curve? Depending on the extent of the
increasing returns to scale, whether it applies to both production
functions, the available factor proportions, and the factor intensity of

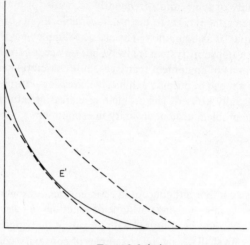

Fig. 10.2 (iii)

the production functions, the resulting production transformation curve may have the normal concave-to-the-origin shape,[5] shown in Fig. 9.2, *or* it may have the shape shown in Fig. 10.2(iii).

Having sketched out two examples of nonconvexity, let us now consider its economic significance. Why does the existence of nonconvexity cause difficulties for our analysis? It is because observance of the efficiency conditions may no longer lead to the realisation of maximum but sometimes to minimum values.

Consider, for example, the isoquants in Fig. 9.1. Suppose that we now reverse their curvature, and make both sets concave to their respective origins. A little experimentation then shows that the locus of tangencies is now a locus of minimum combinations of y_1 and y_2. Thus the rule that RSPs should be equalised in the production of both goods will result in feasible input combinations that yield a *minimum* of x_1 for any given amount of x_2.

Again, in one case of increasing returns to scale, Fig. 10.2(iii), the tangency of the production transformation curve with an indifference

---

[5] The reader may wonder how this case in which both isoquants and the production function curve retain their normal shape can be described as one of nonconvexity. The answer is that with any form of increasing returns to scale, the three dimensional production surface bounds a nonconvex set of feasible input-output points.

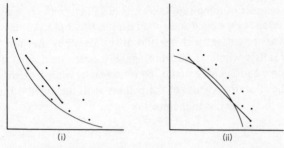

Fig. 10.2 (i) and (ii).   Convex and nonconvex sets

curves at E indicates a point of minimum welfare. The point of maximum welfare is a corner solution at one of the axes.

The conclusion on nonconvexity is this. If isoquants and/or indifference curves do not maintain their normal curvature, (i.e. if second-order conditions for maxima fail to be realised), then adherence to the efficiency rules (i.e. first order conditions) may lead to a welfare minimum rather than maximum being realised. If, on the other hand, the isoquants and indifference curves are normal, but increasing returns to scale prevail, then even if the increasing returns are sufficiently "mild" so that adherence to the efficiency conditions will lead to the welfare optimum being realised, one problem still remains. The set of prices implicit in the optimal solution, if applied to the real world, would entail some firms necessarily failing to cover their costs. This is a weakness in the organisation of an actual market economy, not in the general equilibrium solution itself.

Lump Sum Taxes

In discussing the various complications which call for modification of the simple allocative rules developed by welfare economics, we have had to resort frequently to the device of lump-sum taxes. These have the theoretically convenient property of being able to redistribute income in the desired way without themselves violating the allocative rules. What kind of taxes can satisfy these conditions? The only tax which doesn't violate the allocative rules is one on a good or factor input for which the demand or the supply is perfectly inelastic with respect to *both* price and income. Clearly, taxes on income in general violate the allocative rules: few would suppose that the supply of labour is perfectly inelastic with respect to the wage rate.

Some examples of lump-sum taxes include a tax on the rent of land, (i.e. a site value tax), a once-and-for-all capital tax, and a poll-tax. While these taxes are consistent with the allocative rules, they may not necessarily satisfy whatever distributional principles are desired. If a tax on the income-earning potential of persons were feasible it might combine the allocative virtues of the poll tax with the distributional principles which underlie an income tax.

The Theory of the Second Best

The logic of the theory of the second best can be simply stated. We have seen that an economic system can always attain its efficiency frontier if it adheres to the allocative rules. We have also shown ways by which identifiable discrepancies between private and social costs may be corrected, so that the efficiency frontier may be attained. It was implicitly assumed that all "distortions" giving rise to such discrepancies could be identified and either eradicated or corrected for. What happens if there are some distortions in the system which cannot be eradicated? This is the question to which the theory of the second best addresses itself. The answer, briefly, is that a new efficiency frontier is defined. The conditions for attaining this frontier on which is located the second-best optimum can only be derived when the new system, including the distortion, has been specified. The familiar efficiency conditions are no longer relevant, i.e. even if they were attainable they would no longer be desirable.

The theoretical implications of this theory are fairly devastating. Given that in one sector of the economy there exists some distortion causing one of the efficiency conditions not to be observed, then no simple allocative rules can be prescribed piecemeal for any other sector. In order to formulate the appropriate rules, (i.e. the new efficiency conditions), for a second-best optimum, one must be able to specify all the distortions in the system.

The theory may be illustrated with the help of a simple example, in which there is a single consumer, one input in fixed supply, and n goods. The usual efficiency conditions are derived by maximising the utility of the consumer, subject to the production function, written here in implicit form. Forming the Langrangean expression

$$L = U(x_1, x_2, \ldots, x_n) - \lambda f(x_1, x_2, \ldots, x_n, \bar{y}) \qquad (10.1)$$

and then setting the partial derivatives equal to zero.

$$\frac{\partial L}{\partial x_i} = U_i - \lambda f_i = 0 \qquad i = 1, 2, \ldots, n \tag{10.2}$$

then for any pair of goods

$$\frac{U_i}{U_j} = \frac{f_i}{f_j}$$

i.e. the consumer's rate of substitution between the two goods is equal to their rate of transformation. These are the familiar allocative conditions derived in the absence of any distortions. Now let us assume that there exists a distortion in sector 1, such that

$$U_1 - kf_1 = 0 \qquad \text{where} \qquad k \neq \lambda \tag{10.3}$$

The original optimum is clearly no longer attainable. New necessary conditions for attaining a second-best optimum can be derived by maximising (10.1) subject also to (10.3). Accordingly, let us form the new Lagrangean expression

$$L^* = U(x_1, x_2, \ldots, x_n) - \lambda f(x_1, x_2, \ldots, x_n, \bar{y}) - \mu(U_1 - kf_1) \tag{10.4}$$

Then, setting the partial derivatives to zero, we have

$$\frac{\partial L^*}{\partial x_i} = U_i - \lambda f_i - \mu(U_{1i} - kf_{1i}) = 0 \qquad (i = 1, \ldots, n) \tag{10.5}$$

$$\frac{\partial L^*}{\partial \lambda} = -f(x_1, x_2, \ldots, x_n, \bar{y}) = 0 \tag{10.6}$$

$$\frac{\partial L^*}{\partial \mu} = -(U_1 - kf_1) = 0 \tag{10.7}$$

Moving the last two terms of equation set (10.5) to the right hand side, and dividing the ith equation by the jth

$$\frac{U_1}{U_j} = \frac{\lambda f_i + \mu(U_{1i} - kf_{1i})}{\lambda f_j + \mu(U_{1j} - kf_{1j})} \qquad i, j, = 1, \ldots, n \tag{10.8}$$

Nothing is known *a priori* about the signs of the cross-partial derivatives. It is clear that the usual efficiency conditions will not obtain,
unless both the utility and the production functions are separable,[6] in
which case

$$U_{ij} = f_{ij} = 0 \qquad i \neq j \qquad\qquad (10.9)$$

While conclusions of the second-best theory are unassailable in
principle, Mishan (1962) has suggested reasons why, in practice, their
implications may be less drastic.

Conclusions on Welfare Economics: Reasons for Pessimism

The theory of the second-best proves that, in the presence of any
departure from the neoclassical assumptions, there are no general
allocative principles that can be laid down, which if followed, will lead
to a welfare improvement in the sense of Pareto. Arrow's Impossibility
Theorem proves that it is impossible to devise any minimally acceptable
method of translating a set of individual preferences into a set of social
preferences. In terms of Fig. 9.4, the second-best theory suggests that it
is operationally impossible to determine the location of the efficiency
frontier, while Arrow's theory suggests the social welfare function
cannot be specified. A further reason may be adduced for pessimism
about the usefulness of welfare economics. Its allocative prescriptions
assume the separability of its two component effects—the distributive
and the allocative. But a neoclassical general equilibrium analysis reveals
the interdependence of allocation and income distribution. Any
attempt to move along the efficiency frontier by income transfer will
probably upset the set of prices according to which the frontier was
attained.

A more sweeping criticism of welfare economics is that of
irrelevance: "the major weakness of any criterion designed to rank
social welfare by comparing alternative collections of goods is that of
irrelevance . . ."[7] In a passage which every student of economics should
learn by heart, Mishan continues:

> Once subsistence levels are exceeded, the possession of more goods is
> neither the sole nor the chief source of men's satisfaction; indeed,

[6] A function is separable if $f = f(x_1, \ldots, x_n)$ can be written

$$f = g_1(x_1) + \ldots + g_n(x_n)$$

the technical means designed to pursue further material ends may produce a civilisation uncongenial to the psychic needs of ordinary men. A civilisation offering increasing opportunities for rapid movement, titillation, research, effortless living and push-button entertainment does not compensate for a deepening sense of something lost: of the myths, perhaps, on which men's self esteem depends; of a sense of belonging; of the easy flow of sympathy and feeling between members of a group; of the enduring loyalty that comes only from hardships borne together; of a sense of space and unpre-empted leisure, and of the solidity of the here and now . . . [8]

Mishan elsewhere writes, more specifically this time,

I think it would generally be conceded to-day that questions of stability, technical efficiency, innovation, and the distribution of wealth and power capture the interest both of economists and the public more than do questions concerning the optimum output. [9]

In similar vein, McKean writes,

Economic efficiency, in the Pareto sense, is no-one's first choice, for each of us would prefer to distribute wealth, encourage the use of some products, and discourage the consumption of others, according to his own fancy. [10]

Two general classes of allocative criteria can easily be identified which compete with the static efficiency conditions of traditional welfare economics. There is the class of criteria which is concerned with efficiency in the dynamic sense. For example, oligopoly, an organisational form inconsistent with realisation of the static efficiency conditions, may be more conducive than perfect competition to growth of output over time. In this connection, Dorfman's observation springs to mind, that delegations of foreign technologists visiting the United States seem to be interested in the same firms as are the anti-trust lawyers of the Justice Department.

Secondly, there are selective criteria. Society may decide by selective taxation to encourage the consumption of some commodities like housing and health services, and discourage the consumption of others, such as alcohol. It may also decide to sustain economic activity in rural areas, for social reasons, despite the manifest inefficiency of such activity in the traditional sense.

[7] E. J. Mishan (1969) p. 18.
[8] E. J. Mishan (1969) p. 78.
[9] E. J. Mishan (1969) p. 34.
[10] R. McKean (1965) p. 35.

All of these considerations constitute a powerful argument for abandoning welfare economics altogether, and confining our analysis to positive economics, (e.g. predicting the outcome of alternative policies). Can anything be said in defence of welfare economics?

A Defence of Welfare Economics

In view of the theoretical invulnerability of the second-best theory and the persuasiveness of Arrow's theorem, it is not surprising that a defence of welfare economics must rest essentially on empirical grounds. As a matter of necessity, pricing decisions must be made continuously by public authorities, and the static efficiency criteria seem to be the most "operational" of those which have been proposed.

Pricing decisions can be thought of in two contexts; (1) formulating prices for specific sectors, such as those which are publicly-owned or regulated in market economies, and (2) formulating prices for the economy as a whole, a problem which is encountered in centrally planned economies.

In both cases, it can be argued that where actual pricing policies deviate markedly from those suggested by static efficiency conditions, there are evident losses in welfare. In the private sectors of market economy countries, it may be argued that the market price system operates, however crudely, in such a way as to restrict the proliferation or perpetuation of serious departures from the efficiency conditions. In the public sectors, such constraints are absent. Thus, in Scotland, the very low price generally charged to tenants of publicly owned housing has had the effect of diminishing the supply of privately-owned rented dwellings which in turn has restricted the overall supply of housing.

In centrally planned economies, there was a period when the authorities seemed to believe that there need be no connection between prices and efficiency conditions. No less an authority than Kantorovitch has observed that the consequent losses might account for as much as one third of the value of Soviet output. In the last two decades, most centrally planned economies have moved towards price systems which correspond more closely to efficiency conditions.

11 The Pure Theory of International Trade

One of the simplest extensions of general equilibrium analysis is to the theory of international trade. The theory of international values, as it used to be called, is simply the application of the theory of value to the case of more than one country. The importance of international trade in the theory of economic thought has largely been the result of its policy implications. Economic relations between countries are closely related to political relations: the distribution of the advantages of international specialisation in production, which is the essence of the neoclassical as well as of the classical theory of international trade, provides a fruitful source of political controversy, while the very act of specialisation may itself have serious political drawbacks.

Developments in the theory of international trade have always moved in parallel with those in the theory of domestic values. The same assumptions which underlie the determination of a neoclassical general equilibrium within a closed economy also obtain in the neoclassical theory of international trade. With more than one country, however, additional assumptions must be made; traditionally these are that factors of production and their services are completely mobile within countries, but completely immobile between countries. Transport costs are generally ignored, and other impediments, such as tariffs, are assumed not to exist.

The traditional method of analysis has been a geometric one, with two countries, (one usually designated "the rest of the world"), two goods, and two factors. We shall follow this practice. In the following section we build up a simple neoclassical model of the determination of general equilibrium in a closed economy. This is then extended to two countries, to show how the introduction of the second country affects the set of quantities produced, the direction of the trade flows and the terms on which the goods are traded, (i.e. their price ratio).

Equilibrium Determination within One Country

We begin to build up our geometric exposition with the familiar production box diagram, encountered already in Fig. 9.1. Here, the dimensions of the box represent the quantities of the two factors with which country A is endowed. As before, the sides of the box serve as

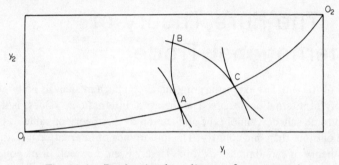

Fig. 11.1   Production box diagram for country A

axes for two sets of isoquants—one set representing the contours of the production function for good 1, with origin at O_1, and the other for good 2 with origin at O_2. Points like A and C are points of tangency between contours of the two functions. The line from O_1 to O_2 joining all such points is known as the *efficiency locus*. To each point on the efficiency locus corresponds a pair of values of the output level of the two goods, x_1 and x_2. When these values are plotted on axes representing quantities of each good, the resulting curve is described as the country's production possibility or production transformation curve. It generally has the shape illustrated in Fig. 11.2. The slope of this curve at any point represents the country's rate of transformation between the pair of goods at that point.

If we now superimpose on the same axes a set of indifference curves representing the community's preferences[1] between the two goods,

---

[1] The community indifference curves illustrated here may be thought of as contours of a community indifference function, which provides a ranking for the community as a whole of all conceivable output combinations. This function, defined in output space, may be derived from the individual consumer's preference functions taken together with a social welfare function of the type described in chapter 9. See Samuelson (1956).

then the equilibrium solution will be determined by the point of
tangency between the transformation curve and the highest indifference
curve. At that point, E in the diagram, the rate of transformation in
production between the two goods, represented by the slope of the
transformation curve, is equal to their rate of substitution in consumption, represented by the slope of the indifference curves. Given
the factor endowments, the technology, and the preferences of country
A, E represents that feasible combination of goods, produced and consumed, which is associated with the highest community indifference curve
of the country. The price ratio of the two goods is given by the common
slope, at E, of the transformation curve and the indifference curve.

By a simple extension of Fig. 11.2, the determination of equilibrium
can be shown in the case where trade is possible between two countries,
A the "home country", and B, "the rest of the world".

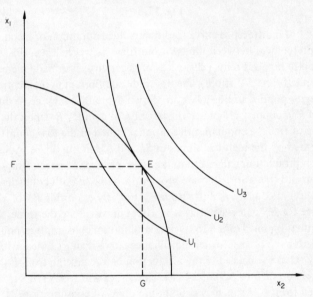

Fig. 11.2   Production transformation curve for country A

Determination of Equilibrium in the Case of Two Countries

In Fig. 11.3, AA is the production transformation curve for country A,
and BB is the corresponding curve for country B. The shape and
position of the curves indicates that the factor endowments and technology of Country A favour the production of good x_1, while the
endowments and technology of B favour the production of x_2. The

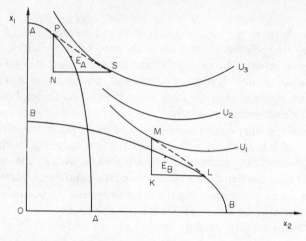

Fig. 11.3

single set of indifference curves represents the assumption of a common set of preferences between the two countries. As we shall see, this assumption involves only a slight loss of generality: it is made merely for simplicity. At E_A and E_B the pre-trade equilibrium points, corresponding to point E in Fig. 11.2, are shown. Note that they lie to the right of P in country A, and to the left of L in country B. Upon the opening of trade, a common price ratio is formed in the two countries, represented by the identical slopes of SP and LM in the figure. Adjustments in production and consumption take place until rates of substitution and transformation are brought into line in both countries. Production in country A shifts from E_A to P. By exporting PN of x_1 in exchange for NS of x_2, country A in effect moves along the trade transformation line from P to its new equilibrium consumption point at S. Notice that S is on a higher indifference curve than E_A. Meanwhile, country B has specialised in the production of x_2, shifting from E_B to L, and exports KL (= NS) of x_2 in exchange for KM (= PN) of x_1, imported from A. At its new equilibrium point of consumption, M, country B is on a higher indifference curve than it was at its pre-trade equilibrium, E_B. This illustrates the proposition that the existence of trade between two countries may lead to a reallocation of production and consumption from which both countries may gain, in a welfare sense.

Figures 11.2 and 11.3 depict the determination of general equilibrium in simple neoclassical systems. The relationship of these systems to those we have developed in earlier chapters can easily be seen. But however simple they may be, they represent an improvement on the classical theory of international trade. According to the classical theory, the identity and direction of the goods traded was determined by cost conditions alone, (factor endowments and technology). But the price ratio and the exact quantities traded remained undetermined in the comparative cost theory. Only when demand conditions are introduced simultaneously, is it possible to determine the complete general equilibrium solution.

A complete general equilibrium analysis of production, consumption and trade between two countries makes explicit what has been made clear in the single country case, namely that the solution is determined simultaneously by all the system's parameters—including the three major sets representing endowments, technology and tastes. Thus, even in the case of two countries having identical factor endowments and technologies so that absolute as well as comparative costs were the same, trade between them could still take place so long as their sets of preferences differed. Readers may satisfy themselves of this by drawing a diagram on the same axes as Fig. 11.3 in which there is just one pro-duction transformation curve, and two distinctive sets of indifference curves.[2] They should then be able to show how a common price ratio may be formed which will make it worth while for both countries to trade, and what are the amounts traded. The equilibrium conditions re-main the same: (a) the equality of the slopes of the trading line, and (b) the equality of the imported and exported quantities of each commodity.

While, in principle, factor endowments, technology and tastes are equally influential in determining the quantities of goods produced, traded and consumed, and the prices at which they are exchanged, modern theories of international trade have tended to emphasise the empirical importance of one or another of these sets of parameters. For example, the Heckscher–Ohlin theorem states that a country relatively well endowed with a particular factor will tend to export those goods which in their production use a large proportion of that factor.

---

[2] By drawing the two sets of indifference curves appropriately, it is possible to illustrate the special case where the preferences of each country for the good which uses that country's relatively abundant factor intensively are sufficiently strong to reverse the expected specialisation. This case explains why the use of a single set of pre-ferences, assumed to be common to both countries, limits the generality of Fig. 11.3.

Thus, the theorem rests its entire predictive weight on supposed differences between countries in factor endowments, arguing that neither technologies nor tastes in practice differ significantly between trading countries. The classical theory argued that the significant determinant of international trade was the difference between countries in the comparative (labour or real) costs of producing different goods. The theory may be given a modern re-statement, in which the significant determinant of trade is held to be international differences in production functions, and that differences in tastes and factor endowments are of slight importance. Finally, it may be argued that tastes are the decisive factor, and that differences between countries in factor endowments and technology are empirically insignificant. There is no identifiable school of thought which holds this last view, but it may, in part, explain the high proportion of trade which takes place between countries with similar, highly-developed, industrial structures.

The Gains from International Trade

It was stated a few paragraphs earlier that the existence of trade may lead to an improvement in welfare for both trading countries. This statement can be expanded a little. It is exactly analogous to the proposition, in the case of a single country, that a movement onto the efficiency frontier from within represents an improvement in welfare. It will be recalled from our discussion of welfare economics that we could state confidently that for any point within the frontier there was *some* point on the frontier which would leave both parties better-off, but that it was not necessarily the case that any point on the frontier was better than any within it.

Looked at from the viewpoint of the world as a whole, or two countries jointly, the opening of trade does represent a movement on to the global efficiency frontier.[3] As we have seen, the "best" solution in

---

[3] Rates of substitution between factors of production are not equalised unless the very restrictive conditions for factor price equalisation happen to be realised (Samuelson, 1948). But allocation after the opening of trade is efficient in the sense that given the world output of one good, the output of the other is maximised under the constraints of technology and factor endowment. The existence of a common commodity price ratio indicates that rates of transformation in production and substitution in consumption are everywhere the same.

welfare terms is to combine this move with a movement along the efficiency frontier until the point representing the desired income distribution, presumably one which leaves both countries better-off, is reached. Of course, a movement along the efficiency frontier presumes the existence of a system of lump-sum taxes and transfers, which is even less likely to obtain between nations than between consumers within one country. In practice, it is most likely that one country A will impose a tariff on its trade with another, B, in order to turn the terms of trade in its favour. While this will disturb the equality of rates of transformation and substitution and therefore move production inside the world efficiency frontier, it may well increase the welfare of the inhabitants of A at the expense of the inhabitants of B.[4]

Offer Curves

Another way in which the determination of a general equilibrium in international trade may be illustrated is through the use of offer curves developed by Marshall from the concept of reciprocal demand proposed by John Stuart Mill.

These can be derived from our foregoing analysis in the following way. Suppose the line SP is rotated in Fig. 11.3. Each different slope will represent a different price ratio and will touch different points on country A's production transformation curve and on the set of indifference curves. The distances SN and NP, corresponding respectively to the country's imports of x_2 and exports of x_1, will change as the slope of SP changes. When these distances are plotted on a diagram such as 11.4, they form the "offer curve" of country A, OQR.[5] Similarly, the offer curve for Country B may be formed, and is represented as

[4] This is another illustration of the theory of the second-best. There is the further problem of income distribution *within* a country following the opening of trade. The Stolper–Samuelson theorem suggests that owners of the pre-trade relatively scarce factor may lose from the opening of trade (Stolper and Samuelson, 1941).

[5] An offer curve may be constructed independently on the axes of Fig. 11.4 in the following way: the amount that a country is willing to export and import at a given price ratio is marked by a point on a straight line through the origin of the figure. As the line (the price ratio) is rotated about the origin it traces out a sequence of points whose locus is the country's offer curve.

OQS in Fig. 11.4. At Q, where the two offer curves intersect, country A's willingness to export OT of x_1 and to import OU of x_2, exactly matches country B's willingness to import OT and to export OU. These amounts therefore represent the equilibrium quantities of the two goods traded, and their terms of trade is given by the slope of the line OQ. The limits of the terms of trade are denoted by the rays from the origin, representing the pre-trade price ratio in each country.

The device of offer curves makes possible a simple illustration of how a country may gain the maximum advantage from its trade with another country if it is able to act as a monopolist. If the terms of trade are not fixed by world market prices, but can be manipulated by

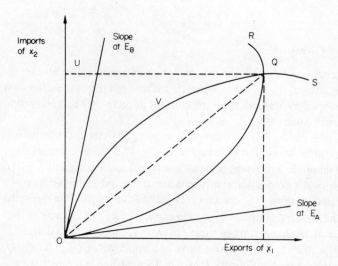

Fig. 11.4　　Offer curves of countries A and B

country A, then the most advantageous trading equilibrium position for country A lies somewhere on country B's offer curve, between O and Q. The new equilibrium position, say V in Fig. 11.4, can be attained by a leftward shift of country A's offer curve OQR so that it cuts OS at V. This may be interpreted to represent the imposition of tariffs or quotas by country A on its trade with B. Where a tariff is used to achieve these objectives, it is sometimes known as the "optimum" tariff.

Many Countries and Many Goods

So far we have employed the traditional device of treating the "rest of the world" as if it were one country. Except in one respect, extending the analysis from two to any number of countries involves no significant changes in conclusions. For two goods, and in the absence of transport costs, tariffs, or other impediments, there will still be a single price-ratio ruling everywhere. At this international price ratio, some countries will experience a domestic excess demand for one commodity and will import it, while others will have an excess supply and export. While the amounts of each commodity exported and imported by each country can be determined, what cannot be determined is the geographical direction of trade. As a result of the assumption of zero transport costs, international trade is treated as though all trade flows go through some central clearing house. The generalisation of the analysis from two goods to n goods involves no change of results.

Conclusions on Trade

Much of the recent literature—both theoretical and empirical—has been concerned with deviations from the standard assumptions—e.g. the implications of increasing returns, monopoly, and external economies, as well as tariffs and other impediments, price rigidity, immobility of factors etc. This has two implications for neoclassical analysis.

First of all, to the extent that these phenomena are significant and not removable, the theory of the second best indicates that the traditional policy prescriptions cannot be applied. For example, the presumption in favour of free or freer trade no longer has an adequate theoretical foundation, and it may not even be possible to argue, on the traditional grounds, that some trade is better than no trade.[6]

Secondly, it may be that these "impediments" are of sufficient empirical importance that they may exercise a greater influence in determining the trade pattern than tastes, technology or factor endowments, identified as the principal determinants in the neoclassical

---

[6] Even if all of the assumptions necessary for the static neoclassical analysis could be presumed to hold there are of course arguments of a dynamic character which might be used to challenge these policy conclusions. Conversely, even if the assumptions underlying the static analysis fail, arguments of a dynamic character may be used in favour of freer trade (see Keesing, 1967).

analysis. In this case, what is required is a new theory to replace the neoclassical analysis. So far no effective substitute has been forthcoming.[7] Until it does, the neoclassical analysis, despite its manifold limitations, will continue to dominate the theory of international values as it does the theory of domestic value.

[7] Perhaps the most fruitful alternative so far has come from Williams (1929) who points out that international factor movements and trade flows are interdependent.

PART III
Classical General Equilibrium Analysis

12 Introduction to Classical General Equilibrium Analysis

Strictly speaking, the Classical school of economists consists of those writers who were the precursors and contemporaries of Ricardo. By classical general equilibrium analysis, however, we refer to that tradition, which, beginning with Smith, can be traced through Ricardo and Marx to Leontief and von Neumann. This tradition is distinguished by certain features from the neoclassical school, whose principal figures include Jevons, Walras, Pareto, and Marshall. In this chapter we shall discuss some of the principal characteristics which differentiate classical from neoclassical general equilibrium analysis.

It was suggested in the Introduction that the classical analysis, as well as macroeconomic and partial equilibrium analysis, could be regarded as a special case of the neoclassical analysis. Starting off with the traditional neoclassical assumptions, one can by simplification and specification of the relationships, arrive at one or another of the classical systems. But classical systems can also be derived quite independently from their own assumptions. The result is that classical general equilibrium systems are less elegant but more robust than their neoclassical counterparts. A possible analogy is the comparison between the representations of the human figure offered by a piece of sculpture and a robot. Generally speaking, neoclassical systems are elegant but not very useful, while classical systems are crude but workable. And they can dispense with some of the more controversial neoclassical assumptions.

The classical economists of the nineteenth century achieved a more distinctive contribution to the theory of growth than to the theory of value. Not to put too fine a point on it, their theories of value were rather crude by modern standards. The twentieth century inheritors of this tradition and the neoclassical school have moved closer together, so that what remain are primarily differences of emphasis, so far as their conclusions about the theory of value are concerned. But they start from quite different suppositions, and these differences are discussed below.

Production Functions

Whereas neoclassical systems are characterised by production functions with continuous substitution possibilities, classical models are characterised by a linear technology. Where there is no choice of technology, i.e. fixed coefficients of production, there are constant returns to scale, and constant average and marginal costs. As we shall show, input substitution does occur in some classical models through the substitution of activities, or fixed combinations of inputs. The consequences are then very similar to those which arise in neoclassical systems.

Theory of Distribution

In neoclassical systems, relative input prices are determined within the system: their value is determined simultaneously along with the values of all the other variables. In classical models, on the other hand, some input prices, in particular real wages, are taken to be exogenous variables. Their value is assumed to be determined by factors outside the system. The classical economists of the nineteenth century thought in terms of aggregates such as "*the* wage rate" and "*the* rate of profit". The current vogue for macroeconomics has allowed this habit of thinking to continue. Yet a fully articulated general equilibrium analysis is concerned with relative wages and relative profits between sectors. A theory of distribution which seeks to explain the aggregate wage and profit rates may be quite inappropriate for explaining relative wages or relative profits, and *vice versa*. The classical economists of the nineteenth century generally agreed on a subsistence-level theory of wages. Contemporary critics of the neoclassical school are particularly vehement in condemning what they call the "marginal productivity" theory of wages. Strictly speaking, wages in the neoclassical system are determined by marginal productivity only in the case where the supply of labour is perfectly inelastic. It is not entirely clear, however, which theory of distribution they would put in its place.

Determination of Output Prices

In those classical models where there is no choice of technology, demand plays no role in price determination. The nineteenth-century classical school were identified by cost-of-production theories of value, of which the labour theory of value is one example. Once choice of technology is recognised to exist, then demand conditions must be introduced in order to achieve a determinate solution.

Intermediate Goods

In neoclassical general equilibrium theory, primary inputs of factor services are assumed to be transformed directly into finally consumable goods. The introduction of intermediate goods does not alter in any significant way the results of neoclassical theory, but it remains true that they seldom appear in neoclassical systems. On the other hand, they tend to be present in most classical models of general equilibrium, and in one, the input-output system, they occupy a central position.

Individual Behavioural Assumptions

Neoclassical theory begins by making behavioural assumptions about individual agents—consumers and producers—in the economic system. Classical systems tend to be more aggregative—starting at the arbitrary level of the industry or sector. The loss of refinement which this involves is compensated for by greater operational flexibility. Classical systems are not so closely associated with particular institutional forms, and may be applied with equal facility to competitive, oligopolistic, or centrally planned economies.

Operationalism

Welfare economics, international trade, and the theory of economic growth are all areas to which the neoclassical analysis of general equilibrium has been extended. In none of these cases, however, have the developments brought the theory any closer to empirical testing. This is scarcely surprising, in view of the heavy demands on data which any neoclassical system would make. It is generally agreed that ultimately a theory must be capable of empirical analysis: a theory for its own sake is of little but pedagogic value. One of the major advantages of classical systems is their relatively low requirements of data for estimation of the principal parameters of the systems.

Determination of Money Prices

In the nineteenth century, the classical school maintained a clear distinction between the theory of value and the theory of money. Attempts to break down the dichotomy by Patinkin and other neoclassical economists have not been particularly successful, for the reasons discussed in chapter seven. Yet recent developments in neoclassical general equilibrium theory have included continuing attempts to incorporate money within the system.[1] Contemporary classical models, on the other hand, continue to deal only with real aspects of the economic system, and absolute money prices remain to be determined exogenously.

Specification of Inputs and Outputs

Generally speaking, contemporary classical models are formulated in terms of inequalities. As part of the solution, those goods which are not produced, and those goods and inputs which are free are identified. Neoclassical systems on the other hand, tend to be phrased in terms of equalities, with a well-defined list of inputs used and goods produced at positive prices specified *a priori*. It is not essential for neoclassical analysis that this should be so: it seems to be a matter of custom.

These differences between classical and neoclassical systems may be summarised in the following table:

TABLE 12.1   Summary of main differences between classical and neoclassical systems

	Classical	Neoclassical
1. Production functions: linear technology	Yes	No
2. Separate theory of distribution	Yes	No
3. Commodity prices supply-determined	Yes	No
4. Existence of intermediate goods	Yes	No
5. Individual behavioural assumptions	No	Yes
6. "Operational"	Yes	No
7. Absolute prices determined within system	No	Yes
8. Number of goods produced and inputs used specified *a priori*	No	Yes

[1] See for example, Arrow and Hahn (1971).

13 The Labour Theory of Value

For the simplest classical model we can begin, appropriately enough, with Adam Smith. He drew a picture of what he called an "early and rude state of society",[1] characterised by

(1) No accumulation of capital.
(2) Abundant land, and therefore,
(3) Only a single scarce factor, labour.
(4) No choice of technology.
(5) All goods yielding positive utility.
(6) All activity taking place in a single time period.
(7) Constant returns to scale and a linear technology.

Smith asked the question: what determines relative prices in such a system? He answered it by saying that goods will exchange in proportion to the quantity of the single scarce factor embodied in them. Since, under his assumptions, labour was the only scarce factor, this meant that prices of goods would exchange in proportion to their labour content. Thus, if it takes men in Smith's model economy 2 hours to hunt one deer and 4 hours to catch a beaver then the ratio: price of beaver/price of deer will be 2/1.

This, in essence, is the Labour Theory of Value. Everyone can agree with the conclusion given the stated assumptions. It is not clear, however, what status the theory has in a world in which there is more than one scarce factor. (Smith himself was ambiguous on this point.) Even if one insists on a single scarce factor, then whatever may have been the case in an earlier "golden age", by Smith's time, land, not

[1] Smith (1937), Book 1, chapter 6. Smith made explicit only the first three assumptions listed.

labour, might have been considered to be *the* scarce factor. Thus the same model could just as plausibly be used to generate a Land Theory of Value.

Intermediate Goods

Hitherto we have assumed that all produced goods are absorbed by final consumers. Let us now introduce intermediate goods. We can do this by extending Adam Smith's example. Let us suppose that this model economy has a third production activity—beaver coat manufacturing—so that beavers are now an intermediate product. If our other assumptions remain unchanged, will the existence of intermediate goods alter our conclusion that goods exchange in proportion to their labour content?

The technology of our three-sector economy is summarised in Table 13.1. Each column describes the (linear) production function for the

TABLE 13.1   Three sector economy with intermediate goods

	Units	1 Deer hunting (one deer)	2 Beaver hunting (one beaver)	3 Beaver coat making (one coat)
1. Deer hunting	One deer	3/4	4	
2. Beaver hunting	One beaver			1
3. Beaver coat making	One coat			
Labour	Manhours	2	4	1

corresponding activity. From Column 1 we read that the successful hunting of one deer requires 2 man hours of labour plus threequarters of a deer.[2] The second column tells us that catching one beaver requires 4

[2] Readers who are worried about plausibility may like to think that some deer are used as decoys. Thus, in a shift of 8 hours, one man using three deer can catch four others. As column 2 indicates, deer are also used as decoys in beaver hunting.

manhours and four deer while it requires one manhour and one beaver to produce a beaverskin coat.

The price of each product can be determined if we establish the equilibrium condition that price should be equal to unit (i.e. average) cost. Recall that this was an equilibrium condition of our neoclassical system (see equation set (5.4)). In a no-choice linear technology average cost also equals marginal cost. Writing p_1, p_2, p_3, for the prices of deer, beaver, and beaver-coats, and w for the wage rate, then this condition gives us three equations, one for each activity. Each equation corresponds to one column of Table 13.1. Thus equation (13.1) states that the unit cost (equals unit price) of hunting deer is composed of the labour cost per unit, $2w$, and the materials cost per unit, $3/4p_1$.

$$p_1 = 2w + 3/4p_1 \tag{13.1}$$

$$p_2 = 4w + 4p_1 \tag{13.2}$$

$$p_3 = w + p_2 \tag{13.3}$$

We have four unknowns for which to solve these three equations so let us, as before, assign an arbitrary value, $w = 1$, to the wage-rate. We can then solve the system recursively with the result that $p_1 = 8, p_2 = 36$, $p_3 = 37$. If we put $w = k$, where k is any constant, we can confirm that the relative prices are unchanged. Our question is whether these prices are proportional to the labour content of the respective goods. From Table 13.1 we can see that if r_{01} is the total amount of labour required to hunt one deer, then $r_{01} = 2 + 3/4 r_{01}$, i.e. 2 hours of direct labour and $3/4 r_{01}$ of indirect labour. Thus $r_{01} = 8$ manhours, and likewise $r_{02} = 36$ and $r_{03} = 37$. These total labour contents are equal to the prices, in the special case where $w = 1$: in general, prices are proportionate to the total, direct *plus* indirect, labour content of the commodities.

The foregoing system can be generalised from 3 to n commodities. In this case, we can write

Price = Average cost

$$p_1 = a_{01}w + a_{11}p_1 + a_{21}p_2 + \ldots + a_{n1}p_n$$

$$p_2 = a_{02}w + a_{12}p_1 + a_{22}p_2 + \ldots + a_{n2}p_n \tag{13.4}$$

$$\cdots\cdots\cdots\cdots\cdots\cdots\cdots\cdots\cdots\cdots\cdots$$

$$p_n = a_{0n}w + a_{1n}p_1 + a_{2n}p_2 + \ldots + a_{nn}p_n$$

This set of equations is merely a generalisation of the set (13.1) to (13.3), and allows for the possibility that each good may be used as an intermediate input in the production of any other. The input co-efficients, a_{ij}, are assumed to be constants.

System 13.4 can be written more simply in matrix notation as

$$p = a_0 w + A'p \tag{13.5}$$

where p is a vector of prices, a_0 the vector of direct labour input coefficients (manhours per unit of output of each sector), w the wage-rate, (a scalar), and A' is the transposed n x n matrix of direct input coefficients, a_{ij}, defined as the quantity of good i required to produce one unit of output of good j^3. Hence

$$p(I - A') = a_0 w \tag{13.6}$$

therefore

$$p = (I - A')^{-1} a_0 w \tag{13.7}$$

Equation (13.7) states in general form the proposition that, under the stated assumptions, relative prices of all goods in the system will be determined by their total (direct *plus* indirect) labour content. The critical assumption is that labour is the single scarce factor. Suppose that we recognise in our system another scarce factor, say natural resources. Denoting the direct resource input coefficients as a_h and writing t for their price, then (13.7) must be rewritten as

$$p = (I - A')^{-1} (a_0 w + a_h t) \tag{13.8}$$

If the prices of the two scarce primary inputs change in proportion then this will leave the relative prices unaffected, although of course the absolute value of the elements of p will change equiproportionately. However, should there be any change in the relative prices of the scarce factors themselves, i.e. in w/t, this will alter the relative prices of the n sectors. This means the end of any single-factor theory of value.

Let us briefly consider some of the implications of a system like

---

[3] The non-transposed matrix A appears below, p. 132. To understand why the transposed matrix is used here, cf. equations (13.4) with (13.9) and (13.10).

(13.7). We have seen that a change in the absolute value of the wage-rate will change in proportion the absolute values of the elements of p, but will leave relative output prices unchanged. This is similar to neoclassical systems, where only relative prices are determined.

A neoclassical economist might object to system (13.7) on the grounds of its incompleteness. No explanation is offered of how the input price is determined. But this is strictly in line with classical thinking: input prices are determined outside the system.

System (13.7) can be applied directly to policy questions. For example, in a centrally planned economy it is necessary to plan a set of prices, and systems like (13.7) or (13.8) provide points of departure for such calculations. In a market economy where a "prices and incomes" policy is in operation (13.8) provides the basis for relating change in primary costs to change in output prices.

If (13.7) has a claim to be a general equilibrium system, the set of prices must be equilibrium prices. In what sense can they be said to be equilibrium prices? As we have seen, they satisfy the condition that price = average cost which is the familiar long-run equilibrium condition of neoclassical analysis. Secondly it can be shown that the ratio of any pair of prices in the set is equal to the rate of transformation between the corresponding pair of goods. Familiarity with neoclassical general equilibrium systems should lead us to expect that the existence of a set of equilibrium prices should imply something about quantities. Specifically, we should expect that markets would be cleared by these prices. System (13.7) however, says nothing about quantities; it deals only in prices. But our analysis of welfare economics revealed that a system which dealt only with the allocation of quantities contained an implicit set of prices. Might we not then expect to find that the set of prices which is the solution to (13.7) has associated with it a set of quantities? Corresponding to this valuation problem there is indeed an allocation problem, which, although closely related, can be solved independently. To this we now turn. We begin with some definitions:

x_{ij} = quantity of output of sector i absorbed as input by sector j

x_i = total output of sector i

q_i = quantity of output of sector i absorbed by households

a_{ij} = quantity of output of sector i absorbed by sector j per unit of output of sector j.

For each sector, we may write the equilibrium condition, total supply = total demand

$$
\begin{aligned}
x_1 &= x_{11} + x_{12} + \ldots + x_{1n} + q_1 \\
x_2 &= x_{21} + x_{22} + \ldots + x_{2n} + q_2 \\
\hline
x_n &= x_{n1} + x_{n2} + \ldots + x_{nn} + q_n
\end{aligned} \tag{13.9}
$$

We next make the special assumption that the coefficients of production, a_{ij}, are constants:[4]

$$
x_{ij} = a_{ij}x_j \tag{13.10}
$$

Substituting (13.10) into (13.9) and rearranging terms, then we have, in vector notation:

$$
(I - A)x = q \tag{13.11}
$$

where x is the vector of sector output levels, q the vector of final consumption, and A the matrix of the direct input coefficients, a_{ij}. Thus

$$
x = (I - A)^{-1}q \tag{13.12}
$$

Notice that, according to (13.12), output levels are determined without any reference to prices. Whereas in other classical, as well as neoclassical systems, prices and quantities are simultaneously determined, in 13.12 the adjustment of supply to quantities demanded takes place independently of the price mechanism. In partial equilibrium terminology, price elasticities of supply and demand are zero. Shifts in demand depend on shifts in output in other sectors, and do not depend on price changes.

System (13.12), together with (13.7), form the two independent parts of the open static input-output system developed by Leontief. We now consider some properties of this system.

The Open Static Input-Output System

Input-output systems such as (13.7) and (13.12) are known as "open" to distinguish them from "closed" systems, where the functions are all

---

[4] This assumption was made initially by Walras, but was dropped in the third edition of his book. Its retention may be justified on empirical grounds. See p. 133 below.

homogeneous. They are evidently static: a closed dynamic input-output system is discussed in chapter 15. The characteristic assumption of all input-output systems is that the input coefficients, a_{ij}, which Walras called the "coefficients of production", are assumed to be invariant with respect to changes in relative prices and also with respect to changes in sector output levels. They need not be assumed to be invariant with respect to time. This assumption may be justified on both theoretical and on empirical grounds.

To a neoclassical economist imbued with the notion of input substitution in response to relative price changes, such an assumption may seem bizarre. Yet a neoclassical system with continuous production functions, constant returns to scale, and a *single* primary input, (or several primary inputs whose relative prices remain unchanged), would also exhibit constant input proportions. This is the essence of Samuelson's substitution theorem, illustrated in Fig. 13.1. Here, the contours of the production function illustrate the general neoclassical

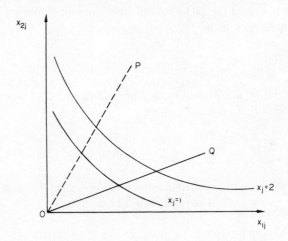

Fig. 13.1 The substitution theorem

case of potential substitutability. But with a single primary factor, only one set of input proportions could ever be efficient, those which produce a unit of output of good j using the minimum amount of the single factor. Thus if the Leontief proportions are represented by points on the ray OQ, those will be the only proportions observed in an efficient economy, regardless of the level or composition of final demand. Alternative input proportions, such as OP, while technically feasible will never be realised.

The assumption of constant a_{ij} may be justified more simply on empirical grounds. The data requirements for systems like (13.12) are formidable but still manageable. To relax this assumption would pose insuperable problems for the estimation of parameters of the production functions.

Primary Inputs and Final Demand

System (13.12) shows the connection between the levels of output of each sector, x_i, and the quantities of each good finally consumed, q_i. By a simple extension, we can show the requirements of final demand in terms of primary inputs. In principle, there may be any number of primary inputs. Let us, for simplicity, choose two, labour and capital, and let us define for them direct input coefficients on the same principle as the intermediate input coefficients we have constructed hitherto. Thus if l_j and k_j are the quantities of labour and capital, respectively, engaged in sector j, then let

$$a_{0j} = l_j/x_j \qquad \text{and} \qquad a_{kj} = \frac{k_j}{x_j}$$

be the quantities of these inputs used per unit of output of sector j. If we form the $(2 \times n)$ matrix F, where

$$F = \left(\frac{a_0}{a_k} \right)$$

then the total quantities of labour and capital inputs required to satisfy any given vector of final demand, q, will be given as

$$\left(\frac{L}{K} \right) = \left(\frac{a_0}{a_k} \right) x = \left(\frac{a_0}{a_k} \right) (I - A)^{-1} q$$

Conclusions on Simple Classical Models

Starting from the simplest assumptions, including no choice of technology, we saw how relative prices could be determined by technology alone. Further information, however, in the shape of demand requirements, had to be specified before equilibrium quantities could be determined. Prices and quantities were determined independently although their solution depended on the common technology. The introduction of intermediate goods and the generalisation to n sectors provide an operational input-output system, but do not alter the fundamental conclusions of the simple model.

However, the introduction of more than one primary input makes the set of relative prices indeterminate, even when the primary inputs enter into production in fixed proportions. And, as we shall see in the next chapter, the simple model is again rendered indeterminate as soon as a choice of technology exists.

14 Classical Systems with Choice of Technology

A Two-Sector Model with Choice of Technology

Let us now return to our simple Smithian world without intermediate goods. In the last chapter we saw that the exchange ratio between the two goods was determined by their scarce factor content. One of the assumptions on which this result depended was that there was no choice of technology. In our model, there was only one way to catch deer and one way to catch beaver. Let us now introduce the possibility of alternative methods of hunting. Specifically, let us assume that when women go hunting,[1] they may take 1 hour to catch a deer, and $1\frac{1}{3}$ hours to catch a beaver. Thus the technology of the economy can be summarised by Table 14.1.

TABLE 14.1   Hours of labour required to produce one unit of each good

	Manhours	Womanhours
Deer	2	1
Beaver	4	4/3

Supposing that the community has at its disposal a total of 12 man-hours and 12 womanhours we may ask (a) what will be the price ratio between goods and between inputs, and (b) how will the inputs be

---

[1] We can surely assume that this was a liberated society.

distributed in the process of production, and what will be the output levels of the two goods?

Since there are only two goods, we can show graphically how this problem might be solved. In Fig. 14.1 the axes measure the amounts of the two goods deer and beaver produced. The segmented line *ABC*

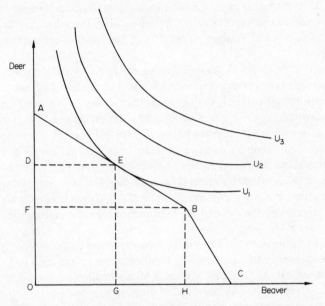

Fig. 14.1 Production possibility frontier for a primitive economy with choice of technology

forms the society's production possibility frontier. At *A*, the entire resources of the society, 12 manhours and 12 womanhours are devoted to hunting deer, the men catching six and the women twelve. At *B*, men specialise completely in catching deer, while women devote all their time to hunting beaver. At *C* both groups hunt beaver.[2] At which point

---

[2] Alert readers will notice the similarity between this problem and the conventional comparative costs illustration of trade between two countries. In that case, it is usually asserted that trade will take place at *B*, with each country specialising completely in the production of the good in which it has a comparative advantage. Since it ignores demand conditions such a conclusion need not generally be true, as the text demonstrates.

on the frontier will production take place? Intuitively, it is clear that the proportions of deer and beaver caught will depend on society's preferences as between these two goods. If society strongly prefers deer to beaver, the point representing the equilibrium will lie on the segment AB, while if society prefers beaver, the solution will lie on the segment BC.

More formally, let us represent society's preferences by a set of community indifference curves, as in Fig. 14.1. Then there are five possible types of solution, depending on the slopes of the indifference curves.

(i) If the slopes of the indifference curves are extremely shallow, indicating a very strong preference for deer, the frontier ABC will cut its highest curve at A. This means that society's total resources will be devoted exclusively to producing deer. At points like A, B and C, familiar notions of tangency between curve and frontier do not apply. Because of the discontinuities, the rates of transformation are not defined, and thus exact equality between the rates of transformation and of substitution is not possible. At A therefore, we can only say that the price ratio p beaver/p deer with be $< 4/3$, its exact value being determined by the slope of the indifference curve which cuts the frontier at A.

(ii) If the slopes of the indifference curves are a little steeper, then one curve may be tangent to the frontier at some point such as E on the segment AB. At E, the society's rate of substitution between deer and beaver, represented by the slope of the indifference curve at E, is equal to the rate of transformation in production between deer and beaver which is denoted by the slope of the segment AB, i.e. $4/3$. Thus, if the equilibrium point E lies somewhere between A and B, then the output price ratio will be $4/3$, and the output quantities of deer and beaver produced can be read off the diagram from the precise location of E.

(iii) If the slopes of the curves are steeper than in (ii), one may cut the frontier at B. Strictly speaking, the rate of transformation between deer and beaver is undefined at B, lying anywhere between the limits of $4/3$ and $2/1$. Within these limits, the price ratios will be determined by the slope of the indifference curve. All manpower will be devoted to catching six deer and all womanpower to catching nine beaver.

(iv) Between B and C, where the equilibrium point will lie if the indifference curves are steeper still, the price ratio will be $2/1$.

Finally (v) If equilibrium is at C, the price ratio will be greater than $2/1$, and only beaver will be produced.

These five cases illustrate the point that the equilibrium price ratio will differ according to demand conditions. More fundamentally, until we have specified demand conditions we cannot say what the equilibrium solution will be, in terms of output prices and quantities. This conclusion differs from that in the last chapter, where equilibrium prices were determined by technology alone.[3] Thus the introduction of choice of technology has created an indeterminacy in the simple classical model which can only be eliminated by introducing additional information about demand conditions. This conclusion is generalised in the following section, but first we should mention the determination of input prices and quantities in the equilibrium solutions.

Suppose equilibrium is at a point like E. Then the equilibrium output quantities and the output price ratio can be obtained by inspection of Fig. 14.1. The associated quantities of the inputs, manhours and womanhours, used in the production of each good can also be read off the figure. For example, it is clear that at E, OD deer are caught, of which OF are caught by men, and FD by women. The remaining womanhours are devoted to catching OG beaver. The total quantity of inputs used will be equal to their supply. This will always be the case so long as equilibrium is on the frontier, ABC.[4] The price ratio of the inputs cannot be identified directly from the diagram, but they may be solved for, using the familiar equilibrium condition price = average cost.[5]

---

[3] The reader should be able to construct for himself a diagram on the lines of Fig. 14.1 but reflecting the technology of chapter 13 to see why this was so. Such a diagram should also show why, while equilibrium prices are determined, equilibrium quantities are not.

[4] Equilibrium will always be on the frontier so long as demand conditions are represented by utility maximisation, and the usual assumptions about the nature of the utility function hold. But if demand is simply specified in terms of quantities of each good, then the choice problem must be recast as cost-minimisation one, where hours worked represent the only real costs. Readers should try to formulate and solve such a problem.

[5] If E is on the segment AB, then the output price ratio is $4/3$. Writing p_b for the price of beaver, p_d for the price of deer, r_m for a man's wage rate, and r_w for a woman's wage rate, and setting $p_d = 1$, then $p_b = 4/3$. r_m and r_w can be determined from the two equations (a) $p_d = 1 = 2r_m$, and (b) $p_d = 1 = 1r_w$. Thus $r_m = \frac{1}{2}$, and $r_w = 1$.

A Multisectoral Model with Choice of Technology

The foregoing problem can be generalised as follows. Suppose that there are n goods, $x_1, x_2, \ldots, x_n$, and that society wishes to maximise the value of total output subject to the constraint that given amounts of each of m inputs are available. Then the problem may be written formally as:

Maximise

$$Z = p_1 x_1 + p_2 x_2 + \ldots + p_n x_n$$

Subject to

$$a_{11}x_1 + a_{12}x_2 + \ldots + a_{1n}x_n \leq y_1$$
$$a_{21}x_1 + a_{22}x_2 + \ldots + a_{2n}x_n \leq y_2 \qquad (14.1)$$
$$\cdots\cdots\cdots\cdots\cdots\cdots\cdots\cdots\cdots$$
$$a_{m1}x_1 + a_{m2}x_2 + \ldots + a_{mn}x_n \leq y_m$$

and

$$x_1, x_2, \ldots, x_n \leq 0$$

This is recognisable as a standard linear programming type of problem, for which well-known methods of solution exist. But before looking at methods of solution let us first of all compare its formulation with that of the two sector model which we have just discussed and with the input-output system encountered in the last chapter.

We have replaced the utility function of the two sector model with a maximand representing value of output.[6] This is a step in the direction of operationalism, for who would care to specify the parameters of a society's aggregate utility function? But it is achieved at the cost of having to take as exogenously determined the prices of final output. Unlike the two-sector model, these prices are no longer determined within the model: they must be assumed to be given.

The input-output system (13.12), of course, could dispense with a maximand altogether, since any choice of technology was ruled out. Where does choice appear in (14.1)? Each x_i may be regarded as the level of output, not just of a commodity, but of an activity or process,

---

[6] By setting to zero all the coefficients of all intermediate goods in the objective function, the maximand, Z, can represent final output, i.e. *GNP*.

producing one or more goods. Thus alternative processes for producing a single good may be incorporated in the system, so that in general the number of processes, n, will be greater than the number of goods.

The constraints are shown as having to satisfy inequalities rather than equalities. This represents a more general formulation than we have had hitherto. When we are dealing with input substitution in the form of substitution between processes each representing fixed combinations of inputs, it may well be efficient for some inputs to remain less than fully used, and for some goods not to be produced at all. It is efficient to do this in the sense that a higher value of total output can be realised than would be the case if it was insisted that all inputs were fully used, and at least some quantity of all outputs were produced. By introducing a choice of technology and an objective function the explanatory power of our simple model has been enhanced. Not only will the solution tell us which of the possible alternative processes have been used, it will also tell us how much of each input has been used and which goods have not been produced. System (14.1) may therefore be regarded as a generalisation of system (13.12).[7]

Valuation and Duality

It will be recalled that the input-output system (13.12) that determined output quantities had a "dual" system (13.7) which was solved independently for prices, but which shared certain parameters with the original. It should not be surprising, therefore, to learn that the allocation problem (14.1) also has its dual, the valuation problem, which may be posed in the following terms:

Minimise

$$V = y_1 r_1 + y_2 r_2 + \ldots + y_m r_m$$

Subject to

$$a_{11} r_1 + a_{21} r_2 + \ldots + a_{m1} r_m \geq p_1$$
$$a_{12} r_1 + a_{22} r_2 + \ldots + a_{m2} r_m \geq p_2 \qquad (14.2)$$
$$\ldots\ldots\ldots\ldots\ldots\ldots\ldots\ldots\ldots\ldots\ldots$$
$$a_{1n} r_1 + a_{2n} r_2 + \ldots + a_{mn} r_m \geq p_n$$

[7] The connection between the equations of (14.1) and (13.12) may not be immediately obvious. However, when primary inputs have been introduced into (13.12), the similarity of the two systems becomes recognisable.

and

$$r_1, r_2, \ldots, r_m \geq 0$$

Here the function being minimised represents the total value of the inputs, since r_j = the price of the jth input. The ith equation of the set of constraints in (14.2) states that the cost of each unit of a good cannot be less than its unit price. If it were less, an unexplained surplus would arise which would not be attributable to any input, and therefore would be inconsistent with a general equilibrium. The inequality permits the possibility of unit costs exceeding price, but in an optimal solution the good concerned would never appear at a positive level of output, i.e. it would not be produced. The economic logic of this conclusion is easily explained. Given the technologically determined input coefficients, costs in a linear system depend on the prices of the inputs, which are themselves determined in the solution. But since a solution requires the maximisation of the value of final output, the price of an input will be determined by its most productive use in value terms. Any good, or productive process which fails to cover its unit costs is absorbing a greater value of inputs than the value it is contributing to output. Accordingly, if the value of output is to be maximised, the good will not be produced or the process will not be operated. In the two-sector model, for example, the activity of men catching beaver was not used in the equilibrium solution. To see why, it is only necessary to compare the unit costs of such an activity with the unit price of beaver. Using the data of footnote 5, we find that the unit cost of men catching beaver would be $4r_m = 4(\frac{1}{2}) = 2$, which is greater than 4/3 the price of beaver.

The complementary or dual condition to the one just stated is that if there is any input whose available supply is not fully used, its price will be zero. This can easily be understood in terms of opportunity cost: it would be foolish, by charging a positive price, to discourage the use of an input where that use does not diminish output levels elsewhere in the system.

The dual valuation system (14.2) is the mirror-image of the primal allocation system. They share the following duality characteristics:

(a) The maximum value of output (Maximum Z) is equal to the minimum value of total inputs (Minimum V),
(b) The A matrix of input coefficients in one system is the transpose of the matrix in the other,

(c) The coefficients of the objective function in one system are the "right-hand-side" constraints of the other.

(d) One system has n variables and m equations, while the other has m variables and n equations.

(e) The signs of the inequalities in one are reversed in the other.

Given the formulation of *either* the valuation *or* the allocation system it is possible by applying these duality characteristics to specify the other problem. Normally, the allocation system is taken as the primal and the valuation as the dual; the dual of the dual is of course the primal. Superficially, it might appear that the unknown variables themselves, (the x_i and the r_j), do not share these duality characteristics. This is not so. It will be recalled that in our two-sector diagrammatic example at the beginning of this chapter, once the equilibrium quantities of outputs had been solved for, it was possible to calculate the corresponding input prices. In exactly the same way, a solution (14.1) in terms of the x_i implies a certain set of r_j. And a solution to (14.2) in terms of the r_j implies a certain set of x_i.

A little reflection will suggest why it is that the determination of input prices and output quantities are inseparably linked in models where there is a choice of technology. Wherever a choice between two alternative processes of production is involved the logic of the optimisation method requires that the more efficient or more profitable process will be chosen. The profitability of a process, however, can only be calculated on the basis of known prices of outputs and inputs. These prices in turn, can only be calculated for a given technology. Therefore, the choice of efficient processes and the set of equilibrium prices must take place simultaneously, along with the determination of the set of equilibrium levels of output. Accordingly, we should expect to find that in solving the allocation system for the unknown set of output levels, the x_i, the set of input prices, the r_j, is simultaneously determined, and this is what happens. Conversely, in solving the valuation system for the unknown r_j, a set of equilibrium output levels x_i emerges as a by-product of the solution.

In a classical system with no choice of technology, such as the input–output system, we had to solve one part to obtain equilibrium quantities and the other to obtain equilibrium prices. But the intro-

---

[8] In a neoclassical system, as we have seen, the solution is simultaneous. In a classical system, a solution is usually reached by an iterative method.

duction of choice of technology brings us very much closer to a neoclassical system where prices and quantities are simultaneously determined within one system. Systems (14.1) and (14.2) are alternatives as well as being duals. All the information we seek can be obtained by solving just one of them. Let us examine the solution to (14.1) and see how closely it resembles the solution to the neoclassical system.

In a neoclassical system, the output prices are those which will clear the commodity markets when the equilibrium quantities are produced and sold. In (14.1), output prices must be interpreted as exogenously-determined indicators of relative demand priorities. The constraint equations require all goods markets to clear, in the sense that the supply and disposal of each good are equal, independently of any particular set of output prices. In this sense, the output levels which appear as the solution to (14.1) are equilibrium quantities. Once these are determined, together with the choice of processes, the quantities of inputs used follow directly from the A matrix. Not all inputs may be fully used:[9] those which are not have a zero price imputed to them. The input prices determined in the solution are equilibrium prices in the following sense. When each input is valued at these prices, the average cost of every produced good is exactly equal to its given unit price. Each input price reflects the intensity of the constraint imposed on aggregate output by that input. Specifically, it measures the increment to the value of the maximand which would result from increasing the supply of that input by one unit. The correspondence between this measure and the neoclassical concept of marginal productivity of an input should now be obvious.

The input prices which emerge as part of the solution to (14.1) are sometimes known as "shadow prices". This name reflects the idea that every general equilibrium solution to an allocation problem contains within itself an intrinsic set of prices. Because of the stepwise nature of its solution, the classical system demonstrates even more clearly than the neoclassical system that relative prices, i.e. transformation, substitution, and exchange ratios, are an implicit, even if unrecognised, part of any allocation decision. The implications of this conclusion, both for the theory of value and for operational-decision-making at the centralised or decentralised levels are profound.

[9] If input markets are not cleared, how can the solution be described as an equilibrium one? As in chapter 6, we must relax our definition of equilibrium to include solutions where excess demand may be negative at zero price. See Fig. 6.1(ii).

We first encountered shadow prices in our discussion of welfare economics. There, we showed how the solutions to neoclassical systems satisfied certain static allocative efficiency criteria. These criteria are also satisfied by classical systems like (14.1). Thus we can conclude that so far as resource allocation within a static framework of analysis is concerned, broadly the same conclusions are reached as in the neo-classical analysis, despite starting from very different assumptions.

15 The Dynamic Leontief System

In the last chapter, we extended the open static input-output system by introducing the possibility of technological choice. In this chapter, we extend it in a different direction. We shall retain the assumption that there is only one production process with fixed input proportions for each commodity, but we now extend the analysis beyond a single period of time, and consider the growth of the system over time. In the final chapter we shall describe a classical system which deals both with alternative processes of production *and* many time periods.

Recall the input-output system (13.12):

$$x = (I - A)^{-1}q \tag{15.1}$$

The number of primary inputs associated with this system are, in general, unspecified. Let us now suppose there are two, labour and capital. Final consumption, q, can then be divided into two categories[1] corresponding to the primary input categories, i.e. into consumption by households and additions to capital stock or gross investment. Building our dynamic model involves "closing the system", that is we treat the output of labour services and additions to the capital stock as being determined endogenously. So far as labour is concerned, this presents little difficulty as labour can reasonably be treated like any other sector of production. The output of the sector, labour services, is consumed

[1] Final demand in static input-output systems is usually broken down into four categories: Household Consumption, Additions to Capital Stock, Consumption by Public Authorities, and Net Exports. In this chapter we revert to our General Assumptions (see Introduction) which rule out the activities of government and foreign trade.

by the other sectors of production, while the sector uses as inputs the consumer goods delivered by many of the other sectors. Just as the production of 10,000 tons of steel requires certain inputs of materials, labour and capital services, so the production of 10,000 man-years of labour requires certain inputs of food, clothing, housing and medical services. The treatment of labour as an endogenous sector of production is very much a feature of classical thinking from Malthus to von Neumann.

Capital cannot, with equal plausibility, be treated as just another sector of production within a static framework of analysis. Labour can reasonably be regarded as a flow of input required by a using sector in proportion to its flow of output during a single period of time. But the role of capital as a stock (quantity) not a flow (quantity per unit of time) in the production process must be explicitly recognised. Typically, production activities require in addition to flows of inputs, the presence of stocks of goods, e.g. plant and equipment, buildings, inventories, which do not alter in direct proportion to the level of current output. These stocks are not used up in one time period, unlike flow inputs, and the same goods may figure in the process of production in some sectors as current inputs and in others as stocks. But stocks must eventually be run down or depreciated, and when they are they must be replenished from current production. The greater the amount of current production which is not used up in the production of intermediate goods including labour services the more goods are available for addition to stocks. The greater the addition to stocks the greater is the potential increase in the level of capacity output. A little reflection will suggest that, with fixed input proportions, full utilisation of capacity in every time period will imply constant proportions of output from each sector. The whole system will grow·at some constant rate from one time period to the next, but the output proportions will not change. These ideas are formalised in the following passages.

We can begin by taking the household sector, (inputs = consumption goods, output = labour), within system (15.1). This means adding one variable, x_0, the output of the sector, and one equation, the balance equation for the sector, to the system. The expanded vector of outputs can now be written

$$\bar{x} = \begin{pmatrix} x \\ x_0 \end{pmatrix} \tag{15.2}$$

And we can define the expanded matrix of input coefficients, $\tilde{A}$, as

$$\tilde{A} = \left(\begin{array}{c|c} A & c \\ \hline l & 0 \end{array} \right) \tag{15.3}$$

Where l is the row vector of direct labour input coefficients, l_i/x_j, and c is the column vector of consumption coefficients, c_j/x_0, where the c_j are formed by dividing each element q_j of q into two parts:

$$q_j = c_j + k_j \tag{15.4}$$

Finally, if we define

$$\tilde{k} = \left(\begin{array}{c} k \\ 0 \end{array} \right) \tag{15.5}$$

where k is the $(n \times 1)$ vector of the residual elements of final demand, then we can write

$$(1 - A)\tilde{x} = \tilde{k} \tag{15.6}$$

$\tilde{k}$ is the "surplus" of goods produced by the system in a single time period which is neither consumed by the production of other material goods nor by humans and is therefore available for re-investment in the next time period. Thus, if $\tilde{k} > 0$, growth of the system is possible.

$\tilde{k}$ measures the availability of goods for additions to the capital stock. What requirements does the system generate for additions to the capital stock? Let us write S_{ij} for the stock of good i in sector j. Let us now assume that the amount of stock required per unit of annual capacity output of good j is a constant fraction, b_{ij}. Thus

$$S_{ij} = b_{ij} \cdot x_j \tag{15.7}$$

Differentiating both sides of (15.7) with respect to time changes (15.7) into a relation between changes in stocks (i.e. flows) and changes in output, viz:

$$\frac{dS_{ij}}{dt} = b_{ij} \cdot \frac{dx_j}{dt} \tag{15.8}$$

(15.8) states that the demand for the flow of goods of type i from current production in a single period for additions to stock in sector j is proportionate to the rate of change of output in sector j. Writing this statement in period rather than continuous form we have

$$\Delta S_{ij} = b_{ij} \cdot \Delta x_j \tag{15.9}$$

The demand for a good of type i for addition to stocks in all sectors is then equal to

$$\sum_{j=1}^{n+1} b_{ij} \cdot \Delta x_j \tag{15.10}$$

The supply of good i for additions to stock is k_i. If the demand is to equal the supply, then

$$k_i = \sum_{j=1}^{n+1} b_{ij} \cdot \Delta x_j \tag{15.11}$$

i.e.

$$\tilde{k} = B\Delta\tilde{x} \tag{15.12}$$

where B is the matrix of coefficients, b_{ij}. Substituting (15.12) into (15.6) we have

$$(1 - \tilde{A})\tilde{x} = B\Delta\tilde{x} \tag{15.13}$$

i.e.

$$\tilde{x} - \tilde{A}\tilde{x} - B\Delta\tilde{x} = 0 \tag{15.14}$$

Seeking a solution to this set of $(n + 1)$ difference equations, we need confine our attention only to equilibrium solutions. In dynamic models of this type, equilibrium solutions require equiproportional growth of output in all sectors, i.e.

$$\Delta\tilde{x} = \lambda\tilde{x} \tag{15.15}$$

Thus we can write (15.14) as

$$\tilde{x} - \tilde{A}\tilde{x} - \lambda B\tilde{x} = 0 \tag{15.16}$$

We can *either* (a) given λ, solve for the output proportions, *or* (b) given the output proportions, solve for λ, the growth rate of the system.

In either case, the absolute levels of output cannot be determined without additional information: only the output *proportions* are determined by the system. The results of two empirical tests of this system, both carried out by Brody,[2] may be quoted to give an impression of its significance. Both tests relied on crude and necessarily aggregated estimates of the parameters of matrixes $\tilde{A}$ and B. Using 1947 data for the United States in a seven-sector model, Brody found that when he substituted the sectoral output proportions of that year in (15.16), the estimated value of λ was 3.92. Repeating the tests using 1958 data for the same country λ was estimated to have a value of 3.78. The actual average annual growth rate of G.D.P. in the United States between 1947 and 1958 was 3.56. Performing similar calculations using a five-sector model for Hungary, for the year 1962, the estimated value of λ was 5.35. The actually observed growth rate for the country's economy in that year was "slightly over 5%".

In chapter 13, we saw how a dual price system existed, corresponding to the static input–output quantity system. We should therefore expect to find that there is a dual price system corresponding to the dynamic input–output system. And indeed there is.

In the static input–output price system, unit price was defined to be equal to the costs of currently consumed inputs together with the sector's value added, i.e. the costs of the primary inputs. But in our dynamic system there are just two "primary" inputs, labour and capital. Since both labour and capital services are produced and consumed within the dynamic model, it is a closed system, and there are, strictly speaking, no longer any inputs which are primary. The cost of labour per unit of output is simply measured by the wage cost, but how is the cost of capital per unit measured? It is simply the quantity of various capital goods times their prices. The quantities of capital goods required per unit of output is given, as before, by the matrix B. There is, however, a one period time lag between the installation of additional stocks of capital goods and the increases in the flow of output resulting from their first use. If that time period is one year, (c.f. the definition of b_{ij} on p. 148), then the value of all the capital goods must be multiplied by $(1 + \rho)$, where ρ is the prevailing rate of interest, in order that the price equation may balance the costs and receipts of each sector in the same period of time.

Thus we have the system

$$p = p[\tilde{A}' + (1 + \rho)B] \tag{15.17}$$

[2] A Brody (1970).

which is the dual of (15.16). In particular, $(1 + \rho)$ the interest factor is simply a dual expression for λ, the growth factor. In other words, the rate of interest is equal to the rate of growth of capacity output. Like the interest rate, the growth rate is defined in terms of a certain period of time, which is implicit in the coefficients of matrix B.

This model of economic growth is an elementary one indeed, and the reader should recall its simplifying assumptions. There is no technological change. The system always works at full capacity in each sector, and output can be increased only by adding to capacity. Each sector increases its output in the same proportion. Despite these simplifications, the model is worthy of study because it possesses many of the characteristics of more elaborate growth models, and yet it can be derived as an extension of the static general equilibrium model, with which it shares several interesting properties.

16 Von Neumann's Model of General Equilibrium

Von Neumann's model[1] may be regarded as an extension in two directions of Leontief's dynamic model presented in the previous chapter. Alternative production processes are introduced, and the possibility of joint production is explicitly recognised. These features introduce indeterminacy into the system which is only removed by imposing a special equilibrium condition or definition. According to von Neumann, equilibrium is a state of balanced growth in which all production process levels remain in the same proportion to each other and just get multiplied by a common constant growth factor in every period of time. But let us begin by setting out the principal assumptions of the model.

Assumptions of von Neumann's Model

(i) *No exogenous limits on inputs of factor services.* Inputs are assumed to be available *either* (a) in unlimited supply, like land in Smith's primitive economy, *or* (b) reproducible in accordance with the technology specified by the system. While there are no limiting primary

---

[1] J. von Neumann (1945). This paper was originally delivered at a seminar at Princeton in 1932, and was later published in German in 1938. It was first published in English in 1945. The paper is something of a landmark in the history of economic thought. It represents the first introduction into economics of the concept of equilibrium growth. It constitutes the first proof of the existence of a solution to a general equilibrium system. And it can lay claim to being the first programming model of an economy.

factors in the usual sense, the treatment of time in the system (see iv below), has the effect of instantaneously fixing the supply of inputs. At any given moment of time, production is limited by the output available from production in the previous period.

(ii) *Choice of technology.* A number of linear production processes are available and goods enter these processes either as inputs or outputs, or both.[2] Thus there can be joint production, and all goods are, in effect, intermediate goods. Each process operates under constant returns to scale.

(iii) *Demand.* There is no exogenous or final demand. As in the Leontief model consumer goods are treated as inputs into the labour supply production process.

(iv) *Time.* There is a sequence of discrete time periods. Each process of production occupies exactly one unit of time, and outputs appear one period after the inputs are used. Thus the inputs of one period are transformed into the outputs of the next.[3]

(v) *Capital Goods.* A nondepreciating capital good simply enters the production process both as input and output. If the capital good depreciates at $d\%$ per unit of time, then 1 unit of the good will appear as an input, and $(1 - d)\%$ as an output.

Formulation of the Model

Let a_{ij} be the *input* of good i per unit level of production process j, and let k_{ij} be the *output* of good i per unit level of production process j. $(a_{ij}, k_{ij} \geqslant 0; i = 1 \ldots n; j = 1 \ldots w)$. Thus process 1 is a way of converting a_{11} units of good 1, a_{21} units of good 2, etc. into k_{11} units of output of good 1, k_{21} units of output of good 2, etc. etc. There are w such processes.

---

[2] In order to prove the existence of an equilibrium solution to the model, von Neumann assumed that every good appeared in every process as either an input or an output. Such an extreme assumption is not necessary in general.

[3] Processes of longer duration can be represented by introducing "dummy" intermediate processes.

Given that the a_{ij} and the k_{ij} are known parameters, we wish to determine the unknown levels of output of each production process j in each period t, i.e. the x_j^t. We assume $x_j^t \geqslant 0$.

The available supply of good i at the close of period t is

$$\sum_{j=1}^{w} k_{ij} x_j^t \tag{16.1}$$

So far as production in the next period $(t + 1)$ is concerned, the supply of good i is thus fixed by (16.1). Any set of production plans which is to be feasible in period $(t + 1)$ must therefore satisfy the following conditions:

Must not

| Total input requirements | exceed | Available supplies |

$$a_{11} x_1^{t+1} + \ldots + a_{1w} x_w^{t+1} \quad \leq \quad k_{11} x_1^t + \ldots + k_{1w} x_w^t$$

$$\ldots\ldots\ldots\ldots\ldots\ldots\ldots\ldots\ldots\ldots\ldots\ldots\ldots\ldots\ldots\ldots\ldots\ldots\ldots\ldots \tag{16.2}$$

$$a_{n1} x_1^{t+1} + \ldots + a_{nw} x_w^{t+1} \quad \leq \quad k_{n1} x_1^t + \ldots + k_{nw} x_w^t$$

In this set of inequalities there are n relationships and w unknown variables. Von Neumann converts the relations to equalities by imposing a further equilibrium condition, which should be familiar to readers of chapter 14. Any commodity for which the inequality rather than the equality holds is redundant, and must have a zero price. But this still leaves us with the possibility that the number of processes is greater than the number of nonredundant goods and we shall not be able to obtain a solution in that case without further information.

The general similarity of a system like (16.2) to other classical models suggests that it has a dual, and we can now make use of the dual to help obtain a solution. Since (16.2) is an allocation system then we should expect the dual to be a valuation system. Earlier models suggest how it might be formulated. Let us write $p_1^t, \ldots p_n^t$ for the prices of the n goods in period t. Consider the operation of the hth production process. If operated at the unit level in period t, its unit costs are:

$$a_{1h} p_1^t + a_{2h} p_2^t + \ldots + a_{nh} p_n^t \ldots \tag{16.3}$$

One period later, outputs appear, generating a revenue from the unit level of operation of the process, amounting to:

$$k_{1h}p^{t+1} + k_{2h}p_2^{t+1} + \ldots + k_{nh}p_n^{t+1} \tag{16.4}$$

Because of the change in the time period, the value of the revenue discounted by one period must be compared to the cost incurred in the previous period. Our equilibrium condition for the dual valuation system states that the discounted revenue from the unit operation of a process cannot exceed its unit costs. Writing ρ_t for the rate of interest, we should divide unit revenue by $(1 + \rho_t)$. Thus we have:

$$(1 + \rho_t)(a_{11}p_1^t + \ldots + a_{n1}p_n^t) \geq k_{11}p_1^{t+1} \ldots + k_{n1}p_n^{t+1}$$
$$\cdots\cdots\cdots\cdots\cdots\cdots\cdots\cdots\cdots\cdots\cdots\cdots\cdots\cdots\cdots \tag{16.5}$$
$$(1 + \rho_t)(a_{1w}p_1^t + \ldots + a_{nw}p_n^t) \geq k_{1w}p_1^{t+1} \ldots + k_{nw}p_n^{t+1}$$

Once again Von Neumann imposes an additional condition on the set of inequalities which reduces them to equations. This time it is that if less than the strict equality holds for any production process, that process operates at a loss and its level of operation must be zero.

Consider as a single system the two sets of equations (16.2) and (16.5). A very large number of solutions are possible to this system. The range of outcomes, however, is further restricted by Von Neumann's critical assumption that equilibrium is a state of balanced growth in which all production activity levels get multiplied by a common growth factor. This assumption means that in (16.2) we can replace x_j^{t+1} by αx_j^t, and thus dispose of the t superscript altogether, since it will be the same on both sides of the relations. We can also drop the t superscript in (16.5), because the constant output proportions implied by the balanced growth assumptions mean that relative prices will remain unchanged from one period to another, i.e. $p_i^t = p_i^{t+1}$.

Accordingly, we can write (16.2) as:

$$\alpha(a_{11}x_1 + \ldots + a_{1w}x_w) \leq k_{11}x_1 + \ldots + k_{1w}x_w$$
$$\cdots\cdots\cdots\cdots\cdots\cdots\cdots\cdots\cdots\cdots\cdots\cdots\cdots \tag{16.6}$$
$$\alpha(a_{n1}x_1 + \ldots + a_{nw}x_w) \leq k_{n1}x_1 + \ldots + k_{nw}x_w$$

and (16.5) becomes

$$(1 + \rho)(a_{11}p_1 + \ldots + a_{n1}p_n) \geq k_{11}p_1 + \ldots + k_{n1}p_n$$

$$\ldots\ldots\ldots\ldots\ldots\ldots\ldots\ldots\ldots\ldots\ldots\ldots\ldots\ldots\ldots\ldots\ldots\ldots\ldots\ldots \quad (16.7)$$

$$(1 + \rho)(a_{1w}p_1 + \ldots + a_{nw}p_n) \geq k_{1w}p_1 + \ldots + k_{nw}p_n$$

(16.6) and (16.7) together are composed of $(n + w)$ equations. As for unknown variables, there are w of the x's and n of the p's, plus α and ρ, i.e. $(n + w + 2)$ altogether. But so long as we are only interested in *relative* prices and *relative* process levels, there will be only $(n + w)$ unknowns. Now recall that whenever an inequality holds in (16.6) or (16.7) the corresponding dual variable must be zero. Utilising such duality properties, von Neumann was able to prove the existence of a solution to a system such as that formed by (16.6) and (16.7). Notice that x_j, p_i and $\alpha \geq 0$, and $(1 + \rho) \geq 0$, although ρ may be negative. If $\alpha = 1$, the system represents the classical stationary state, in which the economy simply repeats itself in each period. If $\alpha > 1$, there is balanced growth, while if $\alpha < 1$, there is balanced decline.

Equality of the Rate of Interest and the Rate of Growth

Von Neumann was also able to prove that if a solution to this system existed then it would be one in which the rate of interest was equal to the rate of growth. We can see this in the following way:

Multiply each row of (16.6) by the corresponding price, e.g. the ith row by p_i. Wherever there is an inequality the corresponding p_i is zero. This has the effect of leaving only equalities in the system. Adding all the left-hand sides within the bracket one gets the aggregate value of total inputs. Adding the right-hand sides one gets the aggregate value of total output. Thus $\alpha = $ Value of Output $\div$ Value of Input. Now, if we multiply each row of (16.7) by x_i ($x_j = 0$ whenever the inequality holds), and aggregate the left-hand and right-hand sides, we find that $(1 + \rho) = \alpha$, i.e. the interest factor equals the growth factor.

What is the economic significance of this conclusion? In equilibrium those processes which are used have zero profits, and must therefore pay out interest just equal to the proportions by which revenues exceed costs. Since relative prices are unchanged from one time period to the next, this proportion is equal to the proportion by which output has grown in one period. Thus all processes which are actually in use have the same revenue/cost ratio.

ρ represents the lowest rate of interest at which a zero-profit system of prices is possible.[4] Likewise, α is the growth factor corresponding to the largest growth rate of which system (16.6) is capable. If not, e.g. if the system were in equilibrium at a less than maximal growth rate, it would be profitable for entrepreneurs or planners to move to the higher growth rate, make positive profits at the given prices, and thus demonstrate that the system was not, in fact, in equilibrium. The correspondence between α, the largest growth factor, and ρ, the lowest interest rate is another example of duality. Recall that in the equilibrium solution to the system set out in chapter 14, the maximum value of Z was equal to the minimum value of Z^*.

The fact that α represents the maximal rate of balanced growth which is possible, given the parameters of the system, means that the associated time-path of consumption is also maximal. More precisely, the path of consumption associated with α offers more consumption in every period of time than does any other balanced growth consumption path. This property is also characteristic of the path of single sector neoclassical growth models which follow the Golden Rule of Accumulation (Phelps, 1961). The Golden Rule states that for maximal consumption, the Investment Ratio should be set equal to the rate of profit. An implicit assumption of the Phelps model is that the capital/output ratio is constant, so that the investment ratio is equal to the growth rate of capital i.e.

$$\frac{I}{K} = \frac{\Delta K}{K} = \frac{\Delta Y}{Y}$$

which in turn is equal to the growth rate of output. And the rate of profit in the neoclassical terminology is equivalent to the rate of interest in the current terminology. Thus, in equilibrium, von Neumann's model illustrates the Golden Rule—the rate of interest is equal to the rate of growth.

The Turnpike Theorem

Despite the neat solution to von Neumann's system, a re-examination of its basic assumptions suggest that some of them appear excessively artificial. For instance, some people may object to the assumption of

---

[4] No zero-profit system of prices will be possible if $(1 + \rho < 0)$.

unchanging technology, reflected in the constancy of the A and B matrixes, over several time periods, while others may be unhappy about the treatment of consumption. These assumptions might be modified without affecting fundamentally the principle of the system. Less tractable would appear to be the assumption that all production and consumption processes grow through time at an equiproportional rate. This assumption appears to be contrary to experience. Then there is the implicit assumption that the historically-determined initial conditions are such as to enable proportional growth to take place at a maximal rate.

The latter two assumptions are not as restrictive as they might appear, as is illustrated by what has become known as the turnpike theorem, first formulated by Dorfman, Samuelson and Solow (1958). They proved the following theorem. Consider an economy with an initial stock of commodities and with its technology described by the familiar A and B matrixes. Suppose the objective is to maximise the availability of the commodities in specified fixed proportions, perhaps different from the initial proportions, at some future period T. Then it can be shown that if a von Neumann (i.e. maximal balanced) growth path exists and if a sufficient number of time periods separate the initial and terminal periods, then any inter-temporally efficient path of the economy between the initial and the terminal points must be close to or on the von Neumann path for most of the time periods concerned. This proposition is illustrated in Fig. 16.1. The broken line in the diagram illustrates the time path of a two sector economy. Ox^* represents the proportions of the von Neumann path, and Ox_h represents the desired proportions of the terminal stocks. The problem may be formulated as one of travelling as far along the ray Ox_h as possible within t periods. x^1 represents the initial input quantities. Notice that the path of fastest growth, illustrated by the broken line, follows the von Neumann path for some of the time periods. The economic interpretation of this solution is as follows. Starting from the initial stocks, the economy begins to adjust its output proportions to bring them into line with those associated with the fastest balanced growth rate. After growing at this rate for some periods, and near the end of the alloted number of periods, the economy once again changes its output proportions to bring them into line with the desired proportions of the terminal stocks. The implications of this conclusion for a country embarking on a programme of long-run economic development are significant. It suggests that in the early stages the country should

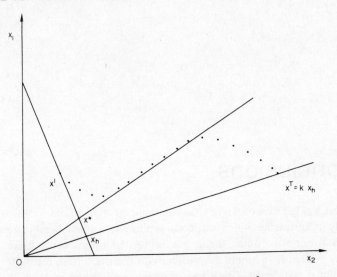

Fig. 16.1   The von Neumann path

try to obtain as quickly as possible certain output proportions amongst its industries and thereafter maintain them. Of course, such policy implications should not be interpreted too literally, in view of the drastic simplifications of the model, for example no technological change, and no foreign trade. However, it may be possible to find in the theorem a justification for the emphasis on the rapid development of certain industries, which has been characteristic of many centrally planned economies. Of course, without having performed the necessary computations, it would not be possible to say whether the sectors chosen were actually those for which the turnpike theorem would have prescribed an early increase in output relative to other sectors.

Conclusions

It was Keynes who observed that economic theory does not furnish a body of knowledge which is directly applicable to policy. Nevertheless some forms of economic theory are formulated in ways which make more evident than others the possibility of transition from theory to empirical calculation. This is true of general equilibrium analysis.

In arranging this elementary presentation of general equilibrium analysis, the theme which has constantly been exploited has been the unifying nature of the analysis. If understanding is the perception of connections between things previously thought to be unrelated, then it is to be hoped that this book may have contributed however modestly to a wider appreciation of economics.

In our discussion of the simpler classical models we showed how the gap could be bridged between theory and empirical analysis. But theory provides a framework from which many competing empirical models may be derived, and indeed there are sometimes competing theories. But often apparent differences between theories are in reality differences in method, so that the theories are complementary, and not competing. This is true of the difference between partial and general equilibrium analysis as applied to the theory of the firm. As we have stressed throughout the book, the preferred approach depends entirely on the question being posed. But we have shown how partial and general analysis are related to each other.

In addition to bridging the gaps between theoretical and empirical analysis and general and partial analysis, the book has also bridged another major gap, perhaps the most confusing from the point of view of a student's understanding of economics. This is the gap between micro and macro-economics. In chapter 8 we have shown how a standard macroeconomic model may be derived from a standard general equilibrium model, while in the same chapter we showed how the Keynesian criticism of the neoclassical theory of value may be formulated in terms consistent with general equilibrium analysis.

The theory of value is frequently taught within a particular institutional framework. Specifically it is assumed that the analysis is confined to an economic system in which resources are privately owned and resource allocation takes place through a system of markets. We have tried to show that our analysis is equally applicable to a wider range of forms of organisation. Even in the extreme case of a system where *all* decisions are centrally-determined, the analysis could be expected to have a computational role in formulating consistent decisions.

This institutional neutrality is particularly evident in the normative approach to general equilibrium analysis, i.e. in welfare economics. There, prices do not appear explicitly in the formulation of the welfare maximisation problem. But in the solution to the problem a set of prices is implied. And it appears that generally in every allocation solution there is implicit a price set, while conversely in the solution to every problem of pricing (e.g. of cost minimisation), there is implied a set of quantities representing the levels of output and the distribution of goods and of factor services. This phenomenon is known as the duality of allocation and valuation.

Finally we have shown how the traditional static general equilibrium analysis may be extended to form dynamic models. These models share several significant properties with static models to which they are related.

General equilibrium analysis thus has a very valuable pedagogic role—it establishes the connection between a number of different aspects of economic theory. It should not be forgotten, however, that static general equilibrium analysis remains essentially a vehicle for the theory of value, and that many important aspects of economics, such as growth and development, money and the trade cycle lie outside its scope.

Bibliography

Arrow, K. J. *Social Choice and Individual Values,* Wiley, New York, 1951.

Arrow, K. J. "Economic Equilibrium", in *International Encyclopaedia of the Social Studies,* Vol. 4, 1968.

Arrow, K. J. and Debreu, G. "Existence of equilibrium for a competitive economy", in *Econometrica,* Vol. 22, 1954.

Arrow, K. J. and Hahn, F. H. *General Competitive Analysis,* Oliver and Boyd, Edinburgh, 1971.

Arrow, K. J., Chenery, H. B., Minhas, B., and Solow, R. M. "Capital-Labour Substitution and Economic Efficiency", in *Review of Economics and Statistics,* Vol. 43, August, 1961.

Arrow, K. J. and Hurwicz, L. "On the stability of the competitive equilibrium" in *Econometrica,* Vol. 26. 1945.

Barro, R. J. and Grossman, H. I. "A General Disequilibrium Model of Income and Employment", in *American Economic Review,* Vol. 61, March, 1971.

Bator, Francis, M. "The Simple Analytics of Welfare Maximisation", in *American Economic Review,* Vol. 47, 1957.

Brody, A. *Prices, Proportions and Planning,* Budapest, 1970.

Clower, R. "The Keynesian Counter-Revolution: A Theoretical Appraisal", in Brechling, F. and Hahn, F. (eds.), *The Theory of Interest Rates,* Macmillan, London, 1965.

Debreu, G. *Theory of Value,* Wiley, New York, 1959.

Dorfman, R., Samuelson, P. A., and Solow, R. M. *Linear Programming and Economic Analysis,* McGraw-Hill, New York, 1958.

Friedman, M. "The Marshallian Demand Curve", in *Essays in Positive Economics,* Chicago, 1953.

Grossman, H. I. "Was Keynes a 'Keynesian'?" in *Journal of Economic Literature* Vol. 10, March, 1972.

Hahn, F. H. "On some problems in proving the existence of equilibrium in a monetary economy", in Hahn, F. H. and Brechling, F. R. (eds.), *The Theory of Interest Rates,* Macmillan, London, 1968.

Hansen, B. *A Survey of General Equilibrium Systems,* McGraw-Hill, New York, 1970.

Henderson, J. M. and Quandt, R. E. *Microeconomic Theory*, 2nd edn., McGraw-Hill, New York, 1971.

Hines, A. G. *On the Reappraisal of Keynesian Economics*, Martin Robertson, London, 1971.

Keesing, D. B. "Outward-Looking Policies and Economic Development", in *Economic Journal*, Vol. 77, June, 1967.

Kuenne, R. E. *The Theory of General Economic Equilibrium*, 2nd edn., Princeton University Press, 1967.

Kyn, O., Sekerka, B., and Hejl, L. "A Model for the Planning of Prices", in Feinstein, C. H. (ed.), *Socialism, Capitalism and Economic Growth*, Cambridge, 1969.

Lange, O. "On the Economic Theory of Socialism", *The Review of Economic Studies*, Vol. 4, 1936-37.

Leijonhufvud, A. *On Keynesian Economics and the Economics of Keynes*, Oxford University Press, London, 1968.

Lerner, A. P. "Statics and Dynamics in Socialist Economics", in *Economic Journal*, June, 1937.

Metzler, L. "The stability of multiple markets: the Hicks conditions", in *Econometrica*, Vol. 13, 1945.

Mirrlees, J. A. "The Price Mechanism in a Planned Economy", in Dunlop, J. T. and Fedorenko, N. P. (eds.), *Planning and Markets*, McGraw-Hill, New York, 1969.

Mishan, E. J. "Second Thoughts on Second Best", in *Oxford Economic Papers*, 1962.

Mishan, E. J. *Welfare Economics: An Assessment*, Amsterdam, 1969.

Morishima, M. "On the three Hicksian laws of comparative statics", in *Review of Economic Studies*, Vol. 27, 1959-60.

McKean, R. N. In Chase, S. B. (ed.), *Problems in Public Expenditure Analysis*, New York, 1965.

Negishi, T. "Monopolistic competition and general equilibrium", in *Review of Economic Studies*, Vol. 28, 1960 (6).

Nikaido, H. "On the classical multilateral exchange problem", in *Metroeconomica*, Vol. 8, 1956.

Patinkin, D. *Money, Interest and Prices*, 2nd edn., New York, 1966.

Phelps, E. S. "The Golden Rule of Accumulation", in *American Economic Review* Vol. 51, 1961.

Quirk, J. and Saposnick, R. *Introduction to General Equilibrium Theory and Welfare Economics*, McGraw-Hill, New York, 1968.

Radner, R. "Competitive equilibrium under uncertainty", in *Econometrica*, Vol. 36, 1968.

Robinson, Joan, "The Production Function and the Theory of Capital", in *The Review of Economic Studies*, Vol. 21, 1953.

Rutherford, D. C. *Classical Mechanics*, 2nd edn., Oliver and Boyd, Edinburgh, 1957.

Samuelson, P. A. "Social Indifference Curves", in *Quarterly Journal of Economics*, Vol. 70, 1956.

Samuelson, P. A. "International Trade and the Equalisation of Factor Prices", in *Economic Journal*, Vol. 58, June, 1948.

Sik, O. *Plan and Market under Socialism*, Prague, 1967.

Smith, A. *The Wealth of Nations*, Modern Library, New York, 1937.

Stolper, W. F. and Samuelson, P. A. "Protection and Real Wages", in *Review of Economic Studies*, Vol. 9, November, 1941.

von Neumann, J. "A Model of General Economic Equilibrium", in *Review of Economic Studies*, Vol. 13, 1945–46.

Walsh, V. C. *Introduction to Contemporary Microeconomics*, McGraw-Hill, New York, 1970.

Williams, J. H. "The Theory of International Trade Reconsidered" in *Economic Journal*, Vol. 39, June, 1929.

Winch, D. M. *Analytical Welfare Economics*, London, 1971.